PRAISE FOR BUYING US REAL ESTATE

"I would consider this the bible for any Canadian wanting to invest in US real estate."

— W. Brett Wilson, entrepreneur, philanthropist, adventurer and "Dragon," and recipient of the Order of Canada

"*Buying US Real Estate* is a must-read for any boomer who wants to spend the next 30 years fulfilling dreams, leaving a legacy, and living a purposeful life."

— Dr. Sherry Cooper, chief economist, BMO Capital Markets, and best-selling author of *The New Retirement*

"This book encourages you to take the time to figure out who you are, what you like, where you will love and what you value. If you ask yourself the tough questions, the odds on finding your passion and living your dream dramatically increase."

— Patricia Lovett-Reid, host of the *Pattie Lovett-Reid Show* and former chief economist, TD Bank

"The book's thesis is that the older people get, the more likely they will buy a home-away-from-home. The spoils will go to those who act in the next two years."

— Jonathan Chevreau, editor of *MoneySense* magazine and author of *Findependence Day*

"Every now and then a book comes along that fundamentally changes the game. This book draws upon real science and substance to permanently elevate the way people and place come together."

— Dr. Paul Stoltz, visiting professor, Harvard Business School

"As a proponent of education and lifelong learning, this body of work represents the foundation for anyone in the world to begin their journey to learn."

— Rod Paige, former secretary of education of the United States of America (2001–2005)

Buying US Real Estate

The Proven and Reliable Guide for Canadians

Richard Dolan
Don R. Campbell
David Franklin

John Wiley & Sons Canada, Ltd.

Cataloguing in Publication Data

Dolan, Richard, 1974-
    Buying US real estate: the proven and reliable guide for Canadians/Richard Dolan, Don R. Campbell, David Franklin.
Includes index.
Issued also in electronic format.
ISBN 978-1-118-43120-7

    1. House buying—United States. 2. House selling—United States. 3. Residential real estate—United States. 4. Real estate business—Law and legislation—United States.
    I. Campbell, Don R II. Franklin, David, 1946- III. Title.

HD259.D65 2012   643'.120973   C2012-905176-4

978-1-118-43978-4 (ebk); 978-1-118-43979-1 (ebk); 978-1-118-43977-7 (ebk)

Production Credits
Cover design: Adrian So
Typesetting: Thomson Digital
Printer: Dickinson

Editorial Credits
Executive editor: Don Loney
Managing editor: Alison Maclean
Production editor: Jeremy Hanson-Finger

John Wiley & Sons Canada, Ltd.
6045 Freemont Blvd.
Mississauga, Ontario
L5R 4J3

Printed in the United States of America

1 2 3 4 5 DP 16 15 14 13 12

Contents

Foreword

by Ambassador Frederick Bush

Foreign investors are investing in US real estate at a record pace, and Canadians are a major part of that trend. Four-plus years of economic stagnation, combined with interest rates at an all-time low and the Canadian dollar at par, have resulted in billions of dollars flowing into the US. Should you join the crowd?

There is a lot to consider when investing over distance. How do you know if you're getting a good deal? What neighborhoods are worth looking at? How can you best manage the purchasing process? The writing team of Richard Dolan, Don R. Campbell, and David Campbell walk the potential investor through all the steps they need to take to acquire property in the US.

Buying US Real Estate is an info-packed road map for finding a property that meets an investor's wish list. The authors have covered the topic from A to Z, including the selection of investment properties, financing and ownership options, legal pitfalls to look out for, and the essential need for proper tax planning, as well as how to carry out renovations and work with a property manager. The authors are careful to warn against buying "emotionally" and provide excellent advice on the importance of investing with one's head and not with one's heart.

This definitive manual is easy to follow and provides the reader with all the tools needed to understand the financial implications of what has to be one of the most exciting real estate buying opportunities ever witnessed in North America.

Frederick Bush served three US presidents—Gerald Ford, Ronald Reagan, and George H. W. Bush—in a variety of roles. He helped found the Canada Institute at the Woodrow Wilson International Center for Scholars while serving as the center's associate director. Frederick is currently an executive with the Vail Valley Foundation in Vail, Colorado.

Introduction

YOUR LIFE'S INTENT: APPLYING THE RIGHT MINDSET TO INVESTING IN REAL ESTATE

As professionals in the real estate markets, we have worked with thousands of real estate investors and businesspeople, and we know that there is something different about the mindsets of successful individuals. They approach life with a certain set of assumptions, enabling them to apply analytical strategies to their decision-making and, as a result, create positive professional and personal lives.

Why is having the right mindset important? Investors the world over are reeling from the effects of the Great Recession. Those effects have, of course, been felt financially, but there are deep psychological scars as well, which have shaken investor confidence. Getting that mindset back, the inner game that is the ability to assess and embrace risk, knowing that some risk is inherent in every investment decision, is what all investors have to work at now. And that mindset is essential if you are going to achieve success in real estate investing in the United States.

We know that Canadian real estate investors like you are watching US property markets and looking for tried-and-true investment strategies. So the goal of this book is to give investors solid real estate investment principles to put into action—but we also realize that giving you this information without asking you to consider your mindset is a lot like giving you a car without a steering wheel!

When we work with real estate investors and professionals, we often hear them say they are "passionate about real estate." Exploring this further (are they really passionate about bricks and mortar?), we find that in fact, it is not real estate they are passionate about, but rather what real estate can help them get. Some reasons are financial—the freedom to choose what you do with your time, time off work, and extra cash flow—but more often than not, their real passions are linked to family, spirituality, or a desire to give back to the community or others who need their help. Using money to accomplish our goals and living according to our values makes us happy.

We share this with you because we believe that it is important that you are very clear on "why" you are buying real estate before you start. This clarity will help you develop the mindset that will allow you to be more focused and, in turn, more successful, and will also give you the mental edge to bounce back from the days when things don't seem to be going right. Time and again, it is the investors who have a clear understanding of why they invest who are better able to get back up, dust themselves off, and move on when a situation knocks them down. In this business, that kind of resilience is a virtue.

The premise of this book is to show you how to use core principles to make US real estate investments work. The subject makes sense because there is no doubt that solid investment opportunities exist in the United States right now that, based on hard market fundamentals, are appealing because of their price (especially compared with hot urban markets in Canada).

But is the fact that you *can* invest in US real estate enough? And does the fact that now is a particularly good time for Canadian real estate investors (or Canadians who want to be real estate investors) mean that you should rush south and pick up a deal—or two or three?

The point is that long before you figure out what kind of real estate property you are going to buy in the United States and map out the road ahead, you need to determine why you are investing in the first place. Once you know that, it's relatively easy to look at the type of investment vehicle that best suits you. The challenge is to recognize how you can fine-tune your goals to hone a business strategy that balances your investment and personal goals. In the meantime, be clear about *why* you want to invest in US real estate, because even the best investment market has risks. Figure out which investment vehicle you really want and be honest about how that decision will affect your life. Real estate investment is an enterprise best focused on long-term wealth, not short-term profit.

CAPITALIZING ON US OPPORTUNITIES

By buying this book, you have decided that you are interested in investing in residential real estate in the United States. You may already be invested in the Canadian market, but you will assuredly find that your experience here is not directly transferable to the US market. For one thing, the American market is a lot larger than the Canadian market—the population of California, for example, is larger than all of Canada! This means that you have to focus on a couple of states and master the investment variables there.

The sheer size of the US market means that there are different opportunities on offer in different parts of the country. In some areas, the best investment play is the buy and hold—with relatively high *capitalization rates* (net income over purchase price) giving the investor steady income streams over the time it takes for property prices to recover and appreciate.

In other areas, the cap rate might be relatively low, but an expected influx of population will put upward pressure on property prices, and property values will recover more quickly. Consider, for example, the almost 34.5 million baby boomers currently living in the northern US states who may be looking to retire in Florida or Arizona over the next decade, when you are looking at investing in those markets.

A lot of Canadians' current interest in US real estate markets has strong ties to the *snowbird* community, that group of retired and semi-retired Canadians who routinely migrate south to escape the cold winter temperatures of their home country. Over the last couple of years, these seasonal US residents have noticed the dramatic proliferation of Foreclosure and For Sale signs, and a growing number are asking if they should be treating their routine US holiday homes as investment opportunities. The answer is a resounding maybe! With US residential real estate prices at deep discounts, can these people reasonably expect to buy a US property, use it personally for part of the year, and then rent it out the rest of the time? If this is what you're thinking of doing, we recommend extreme caution.

DON'T CONFUSE LIFESTYLE WITH INVESTMENT

Residential real estate is a major purchase. However, we see too many Canadians buying vacation property with an "investment" focus, who have no real clue about what's really at stake—it's like a "field of dreams" strategy.

So let's be clear: just because you buy it, does not mean vacationers will rent. That doesn't mean that this strategy cannot work. But it won't work unless you treat it like a business strategy and have a solid marketing plan in place to make sure the property meets your revenue projections.

There are several key reasons why US vacation homes are not as easy to market as some Canadians expect, beginning with the fact that people looking for US vacation property currently have a great deal of choice. Why would they stay in your two-bedroom condo in a gated community for people aged fifty-plus, when they may be able to rent a house with its own pool or a beachfront property?

Timing is another concern that many people fail to incorporate into their vacation-home investment dream. For all of the differences between the Canadian and US climates, our summers and winters follow a remarkably similar path. If you plan to use the vacation property during the coldest Canadian months—aka, a prime winter vacation period—who's going to rent it during the off-season? And there can be other problems, too. For example, the southern United States may be beautiful in the fall, but that's also prime hurricane season. In other parts of the United States, tornado season coincides with prime summer vacation periods.

Another factor to consider is financing. While some American banks will lend to Canadians to buy a second home, your options are limited. And if you are buying property as an investment, be aware that these loans are hard to come by because US banks know that real estate investment looks easier than it really is.

Think about what that means. The US lender is banking on your ability to meet a second-home payment. They think you have what it takes to make those payments. If you're buying that home because you think someone else (a renter) is going to make those payments, be careful. This strategy is not an investment if it puts your lifestyle at risk, so you have to consider that your investment property will have to be financed out of cash or against your existing Canadian property.

Financially, you have to consider your long-range view of the value of the Canadian dollar. Currently at par, the strong dollar makes investing in the United States attractive. If the US dollar increases against the Canadian dollar over time, your income and any appreciation in property values will be in US dollars, offering a higher rate of return. And as a Canadian, once you invest in a rental property in the United States, you are going to have to file a US tax return, and pay US income taxes on your US income. This will be credited against any Canadian tax owing on the income, but you are going to have to hire a cross-border professional advisor to structure your investment so that you reduce liability and US estate taxes.

You should also think about property management, because seasonal contracts are difficult to set up and tough to maintain. It makes sense to factor quality property-management fees into a buy-and-hold investment cash-flow strategy. But if your place is only rented a few weeks of the year, how will you handle ongoing maintenance or repair issues, let alone make sure the place is properly cleaned between vacation tenants? You can hire property managers, but if the property's not renting the way you figured it might, that may not be an affordable option.

From a control point of view, you will not be able to "touch" the property or undertake renovations or management yourself, largely because of the distances involved—much as if you were living in Toronto and wanted to invest in Calgary or Vancouver. The added wrinkle for the American market is that US law prevents you from working in the US without a visa. You will have to rely on American contractors and property managers or become a partner or joint venture with Americans and rely upon their capabilities. Alternatively, you can buy "turnkey" properties from providers, whose business is buying through foreclosure, short sales or "good" deals, and renovating, renting, and providing property management, which makes your cost and returns more defined.

A LONGER-TERM STRATEGY

Let's say that you do a good job of goal planning and you know you want to retire in five to ten years. With that mind, you are looking for an investment that will help make that possible. In the meantime, you don't want to live entirely for the future, but might want to break up the last years of your working life with a few special vacations.

In the short term, Canadians in this situation may want to look at buying a US buy-and-hold rental property with positive cash flow. When you buy a single-family residential investment property in Canada, gross rent is considered attractive if it is 8 to 10 percent of the purchase price, whereas in the United States it is possible to achieve gross rents of 12 percent. These houses should be located in communities where capital appreciation is forecast and where there is an increase in first-time homeowners. As you're looking ahead and enjoying life now, you could use the cash flow you earn to fund those vacations you're dreaming about.

Down the road, several other options may open up. You could use that rental property as your second home, leverage it to buy a second home, or sell it and use the proceeds to buy your dream vacation home. Instead of tying yourself to an investment strategy premised on risk, you've used real estate investment fundamentals to create future wealth and some pretty exciting pre- and post-retirement options.

So let's begin the journey. In Part 1 of this book, we'll look at the economic factors that will affect your investment decisions, as well as our recommendations about the US states where the economic factors are positive. In Parts 2 and 3, we'll give you the ins and outs of buying distressed properties in the United States. In Parts 4 and 5, we'll examine tax and legal issues, while Parts 6 and 7 will be devoted to financing and insurance.

PART

THE DECISION
TO INVEST

1

The Economics Behind the US Market

Much has been reported and written about the collapse of US housing market values. Villains have been identified, bail-outs have been negotiated, and banks have new, more stringent lending rules. Media reports have focused on banks foreclosing on homeowners unable to meet their mortgage obligations, and for families who have lost their homes, it has been a cruel time. There is no doubt that since September 2008, foreclosures of distressed properties have been one of the prime investment opportunities in the United States.

So what is the situation at the writing of this book? Those Canadian investors looking for opportunities in the US real estate market will find that they do exist. But how is the market different than three years, a year, or even six months ago? A lot of factors indicate that while there are still opportunities in this market, they are decreasing. The lesson for the savvy investor is to work fast before they dry up. But first, let's look at some of the fundamentals behind today's US real estate market.

WHAT TRENDS ARE DRIVING THIS OPPORTUNITY?

- Because of the economic crisis, people are defaulting on their mortgage payments and their homes are being foreclosed.

- Homebuilders, bruised by the faltering economy, were caught between slowing business and increased availability of vacant homes; in 2012, for the first time since 2005, US residential construction is expanding according to the US Census Bureau.

- While people have lost their homes, they still need somewhere to live, and because of that, the rental market in the United States is exploding.

- Baby boomers from Canada and the northern states are looking to migrate to warmer states like Florida and Arizona. To put this into perspective, 34.5 million people live in the northern United States and might soon be considering life without having to shovel snow!

- Global economic uncertainty acts as a catalyst for investors to look abroad for opportunities.

NO INCOME, NO ASSETS, NO WORRIES!

The economic catastrophe we've endured over the last few years can be traced to several conditions that combined to make the "perfect storm." One of these was the subprime mortgage crisis caused when lenders gave mortgages to home purchasers, many of whom who did not have the means to qualify. In some cases, no proof of income was required and mortgages were given for more than 100 percent of the purchase price (housing values were often inflated so the banks could lend out even larger amounts of money), giving rise to the infamous NINJA loan (no income, no job, no assets). To make it easier for people to get loans, banks offered forty- and fifty-year mortgages, negative amortization loans, and "no document" loans. In some cases, purchasers were encouraged to add the value of a new car or plasma TV to their mortgages. It didn't matter if the purchaser had a job—the bank was going to loan them the money anyway. Banks put anyone and everyone into a home, fuelling the "housing bubble."

We all know that the sand that the housing and mortgage industry was built on shifted, and the market collapsed, leading to the merger of Bear Stearns with JPMorgan Chase, and the bankruptcy of Lehman Brothers and numerous small US banks. In addition, the US mortgage insurers, Fannie Mae and Freddie Mac, had to be bailed out by the United States government and remain under the conservatorship of the Federal Housing Financial Agency.

When the market crashed in 2008 and the banks came calling for their money, few people had the funds to pay. With house prices dropping up to 100 percent in some areas, the phenomenon of *negative equity* appeared— where homeowners owed more money on their mortgages than the actual value of their homes. Called the *underwater mortgage*, this term became familiar to the many mortgagors who borrowed money, bought houses, or refinanced during the housing boom.

Another consequence of the availability of cheap financing was that builders kept building homes. The end result was an oversupply of houses, especially in the states of Florida, Arizona, Nevada, and California. One of the main reasons for the oversupply in these particular states is that home builders expected baby boomers to move to these warmer states in droves. This over-building was another accident waiting to happen when the crash came, and contributed to the decline of housing prices.

HOW BIG IS THE FORECLOSURE MARKET?

From September 2008 to April 2012, there were 3.6 million foreclosures across the United States. People continue to default on their mortgages, and there are presently 1.6 million more homes in "shadow inventory"—homes that could be foreclosed because they are technically in default. Together, Fannie Mae, Freddie Mac, and the Federal Housing Administration (FHA) now hold over 250,000 foreclosed properties.

At the beginning of 2012, more than 11.1 million US homes (or 22.8 percent of all mortgages) had negative equity, and an additional 2.5 million borrowers had less than 5 percent equity, or were considered near negative equity. The total mortgage debt outstanding on properties in negative equity is $2.8 trillion; Nevada has the highest percentage of properties with negative equity at 61 percent. According to CoreLogic, Arizona, Florida, Michigan, and Georgia round out the list of the top five states with negative equity.

From an investment standpoint, you may be wondering how long this situation can last, and you would be right to wonder. Foreclosure filings for 2012 are decreasing at a rate of 1.45 percent, down from 2.2 percent in 2010, the lowest point since 2007. In addition, the shadow inventory of 1.6 million homes represents a five months' supply, down from 1.9 million last year. What's important for the investor to remember, though, is that prices have dropped by 50 percent and still haven't recovered to pre-recession levels—presenting an opportunity, for now. And while it may sound like there is a lot of inventory around, it is important to identify the "good" foreclosures, where the market fundamentals add up to a good investment.

KEY INSIGHT

Foreclosure filings are on the decrease, which means that this boom can't last forever. With housing prices still below pre-recession levels, now is the time for investors to act.

THE US ECONOMIC RECOVERY

For the last three years, we've watched as the Federal Reserve printed money as fast as it could in an effort to boost the economy. By introducing more physical currency in the world money supply, the net effect is that the value of each dollar is diminished, and the number of physical US bills worldwide has tripled in the last three years. Why would a government do this? Because it forces the value of its currency down while the actual numerical amount of debt owing on the ledger remains the same. The end result is that the government ends up paying off its debt with money that is worth less. And despite the current downward trend in unemployment, and a growing economy that has avoided a double-dip recession, there remains a protracted economic recovery. The constant politicking by both the Republicans and Democrats, exacerbated by the fact that this is an election year, is distracting the politicians from creating real and sustainable economic growth.

Some positive events are in the forecast too. Some elected representatives are trying to help the public, and a bill was introduced at the end of January 2012 to forgive $100 billion in mortgage debt. There is opposition to this proposal, however, and it is uncertain whether it will ever pass. In addition, Fannie Mae is trying to get Wall Street back into the property market by offering 2,490 foreclosed homes for sale to larger investors. (At printing, news reports indicate that the first auction has been held and raised approximately $330 million.) And finally, the Federal Reserve is trying to stem the flow of foreclosed homes coming to market by proposing new regulations that would allow banks to hold and rent foreclosed properties, instead of selling them and depressing prices further.

For Canadian investors, all these factors mean that the door on the foreclosure market remains open for now. But what if any of these solutions, or even new ones, come into play? The market could change overnight.

NEW-HOME CONSTRUCTION

The economic recession has shaken US consumer confidence, but more fragile than consumer confidence is builder confidence. In order for construction companies to build homes, they need customers who can borrow money—and that number has dropped. Builders are also competing with the glut of available homes that are facing foreclosure—they can only build when there is demand. What we are seeing now, however, are builders, who had been on the sidelines waiting for the foreclosure market to evaporate, starting to come back into the marketplace.

The US Congressional Budget Office reported that the annual number of housing starts required to house the growing US population is approximately 1.5 million. Because of the housing crisis, family formation dropped to 600,000 for 2009 and 2010, resulting in less demand for builders' homes. In 2011, family formation increased to 1 million, still below normal. While the drop has caused the "doubling up" of families, it does not mean that the actual demand for housing has dropped—it is just delayed. With the demand being short by nearly 1 million units over the last couple of years, how long will it take until supply and demand come back into balance? We estimate a minimum of three years, and realistically five to seven years.

THE RENTAL EXPLOSION

Another phenomenon has appeared in the wake of the foreclosure epidemic: more Americans are renting than ever before. Morgan Stanley Research, in its paper *Housing 2.0: The New Rental Paradigm* (October 2011), states: "Burned by the worst housing downturn in history, more households are choosing to rent instead of owning a home." According to the Joint Center for Housing Studies of Harvard University *State of the Nation's Housing Report 2011*, "the number of homeowner households decreased by 805,000 from 2006–2010, while the number of renters rose steadily for six consecutive years, up 3.9 million from 2004." In Florida, Arizona, and California, we've watched the share of renter-occupied homes grow by 5 percent.

As we said earlier, people may have lost their homes, but they still need to live somewhere. So, while home ownership in the United States has decreased, tenancy is skyrocketing. In fact, according to Reis Inc., the apartment vacancy rate in the United States has declined to 4.7 percent, the lowest since 2001, and we are in the unusual situation where the cost of renting exceeds that of owning in many areas. We now have a strong tenant market, and for investors looking to get into rental properties, these days are a gold rush.

Investors have been able to buy properties in one of the safest real estate investments—single-family residences (townhomes, apartments, condominiums, and single-family homes)—and earn 6-percent-plus (some as high as 20 percent) returns. This is pretty special, meaning that you don't have to even necessarily factor capital appreciation into your investment decision. The steady rental income from the property provides a cushion, giving you the luxury of time to wait for underlying housing prices to improve.

KEY INSIGHT

The single-family residence is a prime investment, offering a solid income stream for investors, as well as the possibility of capital appreciation in the future.

With the Canadian dollar at par, the largest number of foreign buyers are from Canada, who purchased 24 percent of all residential properties purchased by foreign buyers in the United States. In 2012, 26 percent of foreign investment went into the state of Florida. Other states popular with Canadians were Georgia, California, Arizona, Texas, and New York (Source: NAR). Why Florida and Arizona and the others? For many Canadians, these markets provide a second home opportunity, as well as investments.

Ex-homeowners as Tenants

So, with fewer homes being built, and people needing to rent, where are they going? A brand-new trend is emerging: people are staying in the very homes they just lost to foreclosure and paying rent to remain as tenants.

Let's look at an example of how this works. John is an independent film producer in his early fifties, and is well connected in the movie industry. Over a decade ago he bought a house for $185,000. In 2003, he received a phone call from his bank, and the bank says, "Great news, John! Your home is now worth $500,000. And we would like to offer you a line of credit for $200,000."

Well, John is a single guy working in the film business and he loves his toys. He embarks on a shopping spree and burns through the $200,000 in no time. He's done exactly what Suze Orman, one of the world's greatest financial commentators, warns against: "Buying things you don't need with money you don't have to impress people you don't like." John's monthly interest payments on his home and credit line go up to $6,500—just on the interest alone.

As you may have guessed, this story doesn't end on a happy note. When the markets crashed and the banks called him on his line of credit, John was trapped. His business was in decline, he wasn't making as much money as he used to, and he had no option but to declare bankruptcy. So, at 56 years of age, John has filed personal bankruptcy and has lost his home, not to mention his pride. He put his house up on the chopping block and it sold to the highest bidder for $153,000.

The proud new owner had purchased the home to use as a rental unit. And guess what? He already had a tenant lined up, ready to move in. And that tenant was John. Yes, the very guy who had to file bankruptcy because he couldn't afford to carry the house at an inflated price, with a line of credit he had no business acquiring or spending in the first place. And John isn't the only guy doing this; it wouldn't be called a trend if it were isolated. This story is being repeated over and over again in the southern United States.

By the way, please don't feel too bad for John; he didn't have to move, and now he's paying $1,020 a month in rent, a payment that is quantifiably easier for him. And there's another potential silver lining to John's cloud that works for you as an investor.

If an American hasn't owned a home for over three years and has cleaned up his credit record, he or she qualifies again as a first-time home buyer in the United States. So after three years of good behavior, people are free to apply for a mortgage as a first-time buyer, accessing all of the concessions and incentives normally available only to those making their first foray into home ownership. One of the most exciting incentives for people returning as first-time buyers is the down payment. In many places, it's only 3.5 percent with an FHA-insured mortgage (the FHA is the US counterpart of the Canada Mortgage and Housing Corporation, or CMHC). Americans who have lost a home aren't psychologically wired to stay renting forever. So the one-million-plus people who faced foreclosure in 2010 will be returning to the market in 2013 looking to purchase a new home, and they may as well purchase it from you.

Contrast that with the Canadian situation, where it is still cheaper to rent than buy because of relatively high house prices, and where the interest payments on mortgages and property taxes are not deductible as they are in the US.

KEY INSIGHT

Only in America can you own a home, lose it, and three years later be reborn as a first-time buyer eligible to make a minimal down payment. That makes your tenant of today your exit strategy tomorrow.

PRIME PROPERTY WILL BE IN HOT DEMAND

There is another force behind the major social and economic trends we see, including immigration to the States, called "boomer-nomics" (a phrase coined by William P. Sterling and Stephen R. Waite in *Boomernomics*, published by Ballantine Books in 1998). This is named after the demographic of people, the baby boomers, who were born between 1946 and 1964. This group has driven the economics of every stage of life they are at, from the explosive growth in industries like baby food and diapers when they were first born, to the construction of new elementary schools, to new cars and minivans as they started their own families. Now they are focused on their retirement.

There are approximately 85 million boomers in America and 8.5 million in Canada. This phenomenon is not isolated to North America, as we see similar trends in China, Japan, India—really, all around the world.

Play along with us for a moment and pretend that we are playing a game of musical chairs. You remember this game from childhood, where you circle a ring of chairs and wait for the music to stop, which is your cue to sit down before getting left out. The catch to the game is that there are always fewer chairs than there are players, so people push to grab whatever chair they can, and someone is always left in the lurch. With no chair to sit down in, the last person standing is eliminated from the game.

Now imagine this: you've got 85 million boomers circling a limited number of chairs. And the music has stopped as the first waves of boomers have reached retirement age. What does that tell you? Get in the chair business!

Prices on prime real estate will begin to increase as it begins to be acquired. Growing demand will drive up market value. If this is true, if boomers are going to rush to purchase and live in prime real estate for their retirement, then doesn't it make sense to invest in the places that people are rushing to? And this is exactly what's happening in the US markets right now. The prime spots are going first.

KEY INSIGHT

The US Census Bureau reports that 34.5 million boomers live in the northern United States. What do northern boomers want to do when they retire? They want to get out of the cold. And Canadian snowbirds also want to come in from the cold.

The states hardest hit by the market correction—Florida, Arizona, Nevada, and California—experienced a decline in real estate values anywhere from 35 to 65 percent off peak prices. At the same time, if we look at where retirees have been heading since 1993, we see that these were in fact the exact states that real estate developers were over-building.

What the Bureau of Economic and Business Research Institute at the University of Florida has stated is that 250,000 people are expected to immigrate to Florida annually, right through to 2030. In Arizona, they'll be gaining 1.1 million people in the same time frame, or roughly 50,000 a year heading into that state.

Those numbers are the reasons why builders were keen to develop those areas, and the reasons why many Canadians have been buying up property—because they know that the one thing that is absolutely inescapable is the rate at which we age. Boomers are going to slow down, spend more time with loved ones, and spend more time with their families at a time in their lives when they can afford to. That's boomer-nomics.

In Part 2 we'll look the particulars of the distressed property market, but next let's look at a tool that can help you find the right investment property.

Finding the Treasure with the Property Goldmine Scorecard

With so many properties to choose from, how can an investor decide where or what to buy? Believe it or not, there is a single tool that can tell you whether property in a city or town is poised to go up in value or to drop.

AN IMPORTANT TOOL FOR REAL ESTATE INVESTORS

The *Property Goldmine Scorecard*, a checklist that allows you to systemize your investment decisions, has been developed over eighteen years of investing experience by the Real Estate Investment Network. Set out below, the scorecard can guide experienced and novice investors through a series of questions about a specific property. So even if you don't have a full grasp of the economics that drive the real estate market, this tool will allow you to understand exactly which way a particular property is headed. And you will see how it lays the foundation for investment decisions founded on solid, market-based information, not hype or emotions.

What Do You Need to Do?

Study the Scorecard and Understand the Questions

If you're intimidated by the concept of a real estate investment "system," try using the simple scorecard to analyze a particular piece of property that's caught your eye. If the property earns six checkmarks or more, it may be worth a closer look. If it fails to earn at least six checkmarks, you know your system just saved you some hard-earned cash! Veteran investors use the scorecard to ramp up their "buying machine" and target only those areas with huge upside potential that earn ten or more checkmarks, meaning they have a distinct advantage in the marketplace.

Make Copies of the Card

Practice using the card to "test" areas, so that the questions become second nature. Soon you will start to see opportunities where others don't—by using the Property Goldmine Scorecard, you'll know that certain news signals important investment opportunities. The great thing about a checklist is that it hones your instincts. The more you use the list, the more you understand how the various criteria can positively or negatively impact each other.

PROPERTY GOLDMINE SCORECARD

Property address:

Town:

State:

Source:

Tel:

Property-Specific Questions

❏ Can you **change the use** of the property?

❏ Can you buy it substantially **below retail market value**?

❏ Can you substantially **increase the current rents**?

❏ Can you do small **renovations** to substantially increase the value?

Economic Influences in the Area

❏ Is there an overall increase in demand in the area?

❏ Are there currently sales over list price in the area?

❏ Is there a noted increase in labor and materials costs in the area?

❏ Is there a lot of speculative investment in the area?

❏ Is it an area in transition—moving upwards in quality?

❏ Is there a major transportation improvement occurring nearby?

❏ Is it in an area that is going to benefit from the ripple effect of increase in value because of other economic activity nearby?

❏ Where is the property on the real estate cycle?

❏ Has the political leadership created a "growth atmosphere?"

❏ Is the area's average income increasing faster than the national or state average?

❏ Is it an area that is attractive to baby boomers?

❏ Is the area growing faster than the national or state average?

❏ Are interest rates at historic lows and/or moving downward?

_____ = Total ✓s

Does this property fit your criteria? Yes / No

Does it take you closer to your goal? Yes / No

KEY INSIGHT

Many of the questions on the Property Goldmine Scorecard require you to compare a local area or neighborhood's statistics to those of a larger municipality or state. Your goal? Find the areas that outperform the averages.

3

Let Quality Research
Drive the System

Some of the best sources of information are free. Quality market research is a prerequisite of quality real estate investments, so don't ever skimp on your fundamental research. If you do, you dramatically increase your risk and will likely be caught in deals based on emotions. Worst of all, you could be the last to know the property is a loser—and your own laziness will be your only excuse.

KEY INSIGHT

Never buy a property blind! It doesn't matter who is selling you the property and what story they have told you, it is imperative that you go to the area that interests you and investigate the economics. If you've already got a property in mind, make sure you undertake a detailed inspection before you buy.

GETTING QUALITY INFORMATION FROM THE INTERNET AND OTHER SOURCES

Make sure you get quality online news about the economy. Is the government trumpeting huge job increases (or losses) in your target investment area? Is a new company moving in and bringing employees, or is a well-established one moving out? Have officials just confirmed a new local transit system improvement, or identified where new stations will go? How about a new overpass or a major new residential development? These are examples of the kind of announcements that sophisticated real estate investors recognize as yielding significant investment opportunities. Most people ignore these signs, then call others "lucky" for taking advantage of the investment potential they missed!

KEY INSIGHT

The information you use to assess market fundamentals can come from online or offline sources. But make sure the information is credible, supported by facts, and not written with a hidden agenda.

Don't pay too much attention to the "national average" numbers that are often quoted in the media, because they don't help you to see what's happening in your local area. Relying on these national averages is like saying your head is in a hot oven and your feet are in the freezer, so on average you're doing fine. Your investment decision depends on quality information. Dig deep!

What Do You Need to Do?

Access Local Information

Use the Internet to check out local directories, newspapers, and community newsletters. They will tell you lots of "street" news the major media won't cover because the stories are too local. Crime rates and the locations of busted grow-ops are front-page news, as are new schools and hospital expansions.

Pay Attention to Business Moves

Take a look at who's moving in and out of a community. If a Walmart, Costco, or Target is moving in, someone else has done a lot of research for you. Also, be aware of long-term trends. For Orlando, Florida, for example, you could look at trends in the numbers of visiting tourists. But also be aware that Orlando is more than theme parks, and has a major high-tech business area. This long-term approach avoids the hype and emotion of current headlines that could lead you to inaccurate conclusions.

Study Housing Prices, Housing Starts, Financing, Vacancy Rates, and Other Stats

Lucky for us, the Internet has replaced the need for doing local legwork. In the United States, so much information is available, particularly on demographics, that is not as easily available in Canada. Here are some of the best online sources:

- National Association of Realtors: www.realtor.org
- CoreLogic: www.corelogic.com
- US Census Bureau: www.census.gov
- US Bureau of Labor Statistics: www.bls.gov
- Federal Reserve reports by district: www.federalreserve.gov
- Trulia: www.trulia.com
- Zillow: www.zillow.com
- National Association of Home Builders: www.nahb.com
- S&P/Case-Shiller Index: www.standardandpoors.com/indices/sp-case-shiller-home-price-indices/en/us/?indexId=spusa-cashpidff--p-us
- Fannie Mae: www.fanniemae.com
- Freddie Mac: www.freddiemac.com
- Federal Housing Finance Agency: www.fhfa.gov
- Zip code demographics: www.zipskinny.com or www.zipwho.com

These reports have excellent economic and demographic data, as well as employment statistics. The key is to look for employment-level trends, both good and bad.

Study Demographics

This information will show you things like income levels, levels of education, age, family size, and home ownership by zip code—all data that can help you understand the neighborhood you are considering. You can also get comparatives with other zip codes in the state, city, or country.

Look for State-Wide Statistics

Look at specific information on particular states, cities, and towns. State-wide stats allow you to compare your local numbers against your proposed investment to see if your target area performs better or worse than the average

Use Google Earth

Go to Google Earth (www.google.com/earth/index.html) and have a look at the area you are considering. Look for everything a tenant would want access to, including parks, schools, shopping, and transit. Always locate your target property on the map and see if there is potential in the surrounding neighborhoods.

Obtain Municipal Data

Go online to get a zoning map, a copy of the official community plan, and a copy of the bylaws. Look at local economic developments, like business parks and business incentives to build, which will affect local real estate values.

Check Vacancy Rates

Use the information published in traditional and online sources to gauge local competition and vacancy rates for a particular municipality or community. This data will give you rental market shifts from month to month, and the data is apt to be more up-to-date than formal surveys.

Monitor the display and classified advertisements published in your target area because they will tell you a story you can't find anywhere else. This includes current market data on the *true* vacancy situation, which holds that a higher-than-usual number of rent ads equals a higher vacancy rate and vice versa. Current ads also give you a realistic look at rents in your target market. That information will help you make market-savvy adjustments.

Research Reports by REIN and Other Credible American Research Companies

The Real Estate Investment Network (www.reincanada.com) and other economic research firms release investment information, such as reports and press releases. Get on *every* credible research report mailing list you can find and use the data to stay on top of the latest trends.

Talk to Real Estate Agents

Talk to a number of different agents. Ask to see any overview reports that they produce. Interview the agents you like, then select one and bring that agent onboard your team. Make sure you fact-check all the information you are collecting on neighborhoods.

Visit Real Estate Boards on the Internet

They often have great statistics on current and historical real estate prices, and sometimes the data is free. A good real estate agent on your team should be able to access any of the information you require.

Talk to Property Managers

Talk to several property managers. They can be a good source of information on what's really going on in the rental market. Be aware that many are overworked and underpaid, factors that may cloud their comments, even in a booming market. Others may attempt to earn your business by being overly optimistic!

Sophisticated investors will tell you they won't buy until they've lined up a good manager for that property. So consider this part of your due diligence background work for the next phase: purchase and management.

KEY INSIGHT

One of the differences between buying in Canada and the United States is that for US properties, you have to build a team to help you make decisions—on-the-ground real estate agents and property managers can help you gather and sift through the vast amount of information that is available. Also, you can't work there without a visa, so you need to hire the right, trustworthy contractors to undertake any renovation work that will be required.

INSIGHT

4

Dig for Specific Information and Ignore Generalities

Sure, you can get lucky in the real estate market—many people have. But a lot more have been unlucky. The last thing you want to do as a real estate investor is rely on luck and chance. That's not investment. It's called "speculation," and it's about as good as buying a lottery ticket for your retirement plan. Successful wealth creation through real estate investment is all about uncovering the market fundamentals that can tell you whether a property is poised to increase or decrease in value.

The great news about the American market now is that there is an added incentive to invest: high *capitalization rates* (income after expenses divided by your initial purchase price) mean that while you wait for the property to appreciate in value, you can also count on a steady stream of cash flow through rental payment. Recognize that some areas may be worth looking at only because of the high annual income stream—you can achieve high annual returns but never see appreciation in value of the property itself—and you have to be satisfied that the high income will offset the requirement for appreciation.

THE MARKET TODAY AND TOMORROW

You're looking for markets with a future, not a past. A town or neighborhood may show rising values today, but sophisticated investors look at how it will perform in the future. Please note that we are talking about specific town or neighborhood research, not market generalities. General state or national real estate stats mean nothing to a sophisticated investor. Sure, they're interesting to read, but they're useless to an investor because they don't drill down into a specific target area.

For example, you may hear a media report that the average national or state real estate values increased by 5 percent year over year. That number is generally useless. It could mean that some markets are up 10 percent, while others are down 5 percent, thus averaging 5 percent. If you base your investment decisions on such a general number, you might say, "Great, real estate prices are up again, so let's buy some more." But if you're not paying attention to local numbers, you could be the one buying in a region where prices are dropping.

What Do You Need to Do?

Understand the Two Types of Fundamentals

Some market fundamentals are passive, meaning they're outside the investor's control. Passive fundamentals often have the largest impact on the long-term value of your properties. A major example that will impact Florida and Arizona in particular is based on the aging demographics of the US population—remember those baby boomers living in the northern United States who might want to retire in the sun.

Other fundamentals are within the investor's control, such as "sweat equity." The key is to find properties where you have a combination of both. You need to understand how both kinds of factors impact the investment environment.

KEY INSIGHT

Build your portfolio on a strong foundation of fundamentals and it will create long-term wealth. Build it on hype and poor fundamentals and it becomes higher risk and could invite financial disaster.

WARNING

Don't just buy any property in a region that offers great fundamentals. The property must also fit detailed investment criteria. Not all properties will work, even if the fundamentals are there.

Consider Passive and Active Factors

Passive factors: indicators of future strength

These factors wield a direct influence on market strength, but are outside an investor's control:

- Mortgage interest rates

- Wealth effect

- Affordability index

- Increased job growth

- Boom effect

- Infrastructure expansion

- Gentrification and renewal

- Overall economic outlook

- Employment rates

- Industry and commerce

Active factors: areas you can control

Market-savvy investors know these factors help them boost investment value:

- Maximizing zoning and value

- Direct renovations

- Curb appeal

- Divide and profit

- Speculation on tips.

5

Jobs, Infrastructure, and Gentrification

When companies or governments make major announcements of new jobs or new business relocations, they trigger a significant increase in housing demand. Naturally, the housing supply takes time to catch up to this demand, but often never does. From this increased demand and fixed supply, real estate prices get driven up in a given area more quickly than the regional average.

SIGNS OF POTENTIAL ECONOMIC GROWTH

Savvy real estate investors know it pays to read the newspaper and Internet news. Always be on the lookout for major announcements of new jobs, major expansions, or new employers moving into an area. Look for areas where people are moving to fill tremendous job opportunities—a good sign of a potential increase in residential housing demand.

What Do You Need to Do?

Look for Jobs, Jobs, Jobs

When analyzing a region, look for cities, towns, and neighborhoods in high demand because of what's happening in the local labor market in terms of an increase in jobs or easier access to jobs. You can see this in Miami, for example, where there are plans for a major casino development.

Your goal is to find areas where the population is growing faster than the national average due to an influx of jobs. In some towns, the population will be growing because the town has become a retirement haven or is a cheap place to live, but this does not always lead to increased real estate values. You want to find cities, towns, and neighborhoods that are gaining reputations as great places to live and have a growing economy.

Study Both Components of New Residents

People moving into a town to fill new jobs come from two main sources: *immigration* occurs when people move from other countries into a new country; *intra-migration* occurs when people move from one part of the country to another. People, generally speaking, look for rental properties until they are settled, which usually takes about two years. After two years, those with savings look to buy a home, so investors win in both cases. They have a market for their rentals and a stable market for the properties they wish to sell in the future.

These sources of migration can exist independently of each other, or combine to provide a very strong market. What you'll generally find is that if a region is creating a lot more jobs than the average, the immigration and intra-migration numbers will be very strong. As people migrate to your target region, you will need to make adjustments to your marketing plan. Make sure you know which type of migration your plan will focus on. Again, consider the example of the Miami market, where a huge influx of South American buyers is stabilizing housing prices.

WARNING

If you discover you have targeted a region where there is a net loss of intra-migration and/or immigration, seriously reconsider any long-term real estate investments there. You will find that your market will shrink while available housing units increase, and less demand + fixed supply = decreasing prices.

BUSINESS-FRIENDLY POLICIES ARE VITAL

Real estate investment is a complicated business impacted by local economic developments. In a perfect investment world, you want to invest in an area with the potential to attract and sustain a good supply of quality renters and eventual buyers. That means an area with strong economic growth potential in terms of new industries and new jobs. It also means finding a business-friendly environment with minimal taxation (personal and property) and with a fair landlord–tenant law structure.

If you find a region with a dynamic, forward-looking economic development plan, you have just identified an area that has a great potential for attracting employers. If you wish to be successful in the business of real estate investing, you want to have a business-friendly atmosphere that is designed to attract people. You want a town or city that promotes itself and actively attracts investment, as this will help your business succeed. Real estate investing is a business, so you want to look for business-friendly atmospheres.

A macro-level analysis of a state's tax and tenant laws is just the beginning. You will find states and municipalities that offer distinct advantages in both of these areas. You also must look at local tax structures for both business and property.

What Do You Need to Do?

Get Involved

Join the local landlord association and/or a local real estate investment network. Through the association you will have access to the decision-makers and be able to keep your finger on the pulse of your target investment region.

Do Your Homework

Find out why nearly identical properties in different communities are priced differently. Get your information from people who live and work in the community, including real estate agents.

Take a look at how local tenancy laws impact the region's real estate investment opportunities and learn how actual or proposed zoning bylaws can nourish or strangle local property values. Consider taxes on rental income from residential property payable in Arizona and Florida.

TRAINS, PLANES, AUTOMOBILES: INFRASTRUCTURE MATTERS

Access, access, access—that's all that matters. Paying attention will pay you dividends. When you read an announcement of a major infrastructure improvement in the works, get off your couch and check it out, using the "what's behind the curtain?" approach to analyze the potential benefits.

Examples could include an announcement that the city has annexed new land, news of a new transportation development, or a new sewer or water plant—all of which show signs of a region looking forward to growth potential.

KEY INSIGHT

Picture an area near your region that is currently serviced by a highway. Now take away that highway and picture how that would affect access to the region—and its desirability. In most, if not all, cases, you will see that the region could never have grown to its current status without transportation infrastructure.

Once the transportation improvement is completed, the serviced region will grow at a much faster rate. Proximity to light-rail transportation commuting routes, for example, pushes property values up by giving commuters better access to the downtown core. Demand for real estate will increase, more jobs will move to the region and, best of all, people will follow. This is just one of many infrastructure improvements you can take advantage of.

It is not just new transportation that drives these values. Watch for widening of highways and the construction of highway extensions and overpasses. These infrastructure changes will reduce commuting times and push up property values and rents.

What Do You Need to Do?

Keep Informed

Read the major media; watch for any announcement of major infrastructure improvements in your target investment region. These will identify a region that is set to grow when other regions are in stasis or decline. Read the local press of the region you are targeting for investment, as often this is where the real gems are found.

Analyze a Neighborhood as If It were a Town on Its Own

Ask yourself a few questions: Where do the people who live here work? Is the investment value of residential property recognized and respected by municipal leaders when they make decisions about area roads and land use changes? What will the demand be like when the infrastructure improvement is completed?

KEY INSIGHT

Governments like to announce, then re-announce and re-announce again, infrastructure improvement projects. Never invest based solely on announcements—many projects never come to fruition. Sophisticated investors wait until they "see the smoke." In other words, they wait to see the project actually being worked on, making it less likely to stop.

GENTRIFICATION AND RENEWAL

Is it shabby or chic? Watch for clues that show a neighborhood is moving from one economic class to the next. Often described as tough but funky, older neighborhoods that turn into good investment opportunities typically start as working-class communities on the "outskirts" of a more central hub. Many feature once well-kept homes that slid into disrepair—and out of residential real estate favor—as suburban neighborhoods sprouted in the 1970s and 1980s.

What Do You Need to Do?
Know the Signs

These days, these regions are easy to recognize. They tend to have a few houses that show signs of recent renovation, located alongside a mix of older, unrenovated character homes. These regions often turn into great family neighborhoods, as they have larger lots or older landscaping, and are close to transit or job locations.

Visit Neighborhoods in Person

Before you invest in these renewal areas, you *must* drive through them to look for signs of increasing pride of ownership. These include tended gardens, new paint or siding being added to properties, and newer cars in the driveways. These properties will be surrounded by others that have not yet begun this transition, and these are your target properties. Look at what has occurred in the Junction area of Toronto, the inner city of

Calgary, or the Yaletown neighborhood in Vancouver to see the real impact of this factor.

KEY INSIGHT

Never buy the best property in the neighborhood. Buy the worst and bring it up to the neighborhood benchmark and you will get the biggest bang for your investment dollar. And never be the first to invest in a renewal area, as sometimes the gentrification doesn't fully take hold and neglect still characterizes the neighborhood. To reduce the risk, wait for the renewal to really take hold.

These transitional neighborhoods aren't all located just outside of a community's "inner core." Some of these neighborhoods are right downtown, where old, run-down warehouses are being refurbished as apartments or upscale luxury condominium lofts.

In other regions, look for dilapidated industrial buildings that are being torn down or renovated. These include in-fill developments, where developers knock down old buildings and construct narrow, zero-lot-line houses or townhouses.

KEY INSIGHT

You can use these redevelopments as part of your boom effect fundamental strategy. As the region's older industrial buildings are redeveloped, the areas surrounding them will dramatically increase in demand.

Look for Clues

How do you know if you've caught the neighborhood at the right time? Look for tell-tale signs of continued improvement. These include a mixture of older model cars and new vehicles. The gentrification is more advanced if the number of new cars has outstripped older models.

Look for media stories about neighborhoods whose property owners talk about "taking back" their neighborhood from prostitutes and drug dealers. Meet with the local Neighborhood Watch or community group to see what's going on and where they want to take the community. Invest in regions where the leadership is strong and they want to renew their neighborhood.

Exercise Prudent Patience

Renewal areas have long-term profit potential. But you do *not* want to be the first investor in an area you believe is going to be in transition.

When you invest in a neighborhood where renewal has begun, it often means you are buying into a neighborhood with a more transient tenant profile and lower-than-average rents. The tenant situation will improve and the values increase as the renewal progresses, but it will take time. You will need patience to buy in transition areas.

KEY INSIGHT

Local investors are often the last to discover neighborhoods going through the process of renewal. That's because they let their personal beliefs about where they would live obscure the fundamentals of their investment system. They let their emotions and past history affect their investments. This is an example of what goes wrong when you make decisions based on emotions instead of facts—you miss the biggest opportunities.

6

A Closer Look at Three States

We have established that the United States is a huge market, and have looked at the kinds of factors that you should take into account by using the Property Goldmine Scorecard before you invest. But given the size of the marketplace and the number of opportunities available, where should you buy?

As a first step, you may be interested in where your fellow foreign investors are buying. According to the National Association of Realtors, the following are the top states where foreigners are buying: Florida 26 percent; California 11 percent; then Texas and Arizona tied at 7 percent; and two states tied at 4 percent, New York and Georgia—59 percent of the total foreign purchases invested in six states.

Here we show you how to look at economic information to decide where to invest. We've done our homework, and these are the three states that we think show the most promise these days.

FLORIDA

If you live in Canada, then it's no surprise that Florida is one of the most popular destinations for Canadians—especially those of us from the eastern part of the country. Ease of travel has played a large part in this, as has the weather of course, especially in the winter months from November to March.

More than a vacation destination, however, Florida also stands up as a great second-home destination for Canadians. In the past, a second home was something that only wealthy people could afford due in part to the exchange rate—remember the days when you needed C$1.62 to buy US$1?

Well, with the Canadian dollar at par, that has completely reversed, making US property that much more affordable.

So where did Canadians invest in Florida? The top destinations in 2011 for Canadian homebuyers and investors were Tampa/St Petersburg/Clearwater (17 percent); Miami/Fort Lauderdale/Miami Beach (15 percent); Orlando/Kissimmee (14 percent); Naples/Marco Island (10 percent); and Cape Coral/Fort Myers (10 percent). The rest of the state accounts for less than 35 percent of the Canadian money flowing into Florida.

Housing Prices Rising

Fuelled by foreign investment from Canada and Brazil, Florida has experienced a 4.7 percent increase in residential home prices. What is happening in Florida has surprised many Canadians who believe the United States is still on sale and there is a huge supply of homes waiting for them to purchase. As the trend in rising prices continues, it is and will become harder and harder to buy an investment property in Florida at a discounted price.

According to the Zillow Home Value Index, the high median price for the state of Florida as a whole was $264,000 in April 2006. The low median price of $120,000 was hit in September 2011. This is starting to recover, and as of March 2012, the index stood at $122,000.

The following statistics, courtesy of Trulia, show the median sale price trends in specific cities in Florida over the last six months.

City	Peak Median Price	Low Median Price	Median Price May 2012
Miami	$315k	$114k	$155k
Fort Lauderdale	$347k	$120k	$176k
Orlando	$255k	$80k	$110k
Naples	$391k	$142k	$200k
Boca Raton	$388k	$152k	$177k
Sarasota	$305k	$125k	$176k
St Petersburg	$184k	$70k	$87k
Clearwater	$210k	$86k	$90k
Cape Coral	$255k	$87k	$115k

One reason Florida is attractive to international investors is that it has no state income tax. In addition, Florida has a low land-transfer tax, averaging

0.7 percent average for the state, with Miami-Dade County at 0.6 percent and 0.35 percent per thousand for the registration of a mortgage. Contrast this with New York, where the land transfer tax is 4 percent plus 1 percent per thousand for homes in excess of $1 million; 5.1 percent per thousand for Las Vegas; 16.01 percent for Berkeley in Oakland, California; and 4.4 percent per thousand for Los Angeles. In addition, these states have state income taxes of up to 8.82 percent in New York and 9.3 percent in California.

The March 2012 report from CoreLogic states that the foreclosure inventory in Florida is 12 percent of all homes, and 17.4 percent of all mortgaged homes are in ninety-day-plus delinquency. Moreover, CoreLogic's *Report on Negative Equity,* released in March 2012, stated that 44.2 percent of mortgaged homes in Florida were in negative equity territory. To put this in perspective, consider that the prices in Florida are increasing strongly in spite of this statistic. The positive force in this market is tremendously powerful, and is clearly overriding some of the unflattering statistics.

In Miami, there are twenty-four new condominium projects underway as of the writing of this book. That's because there is demand—developers would not consider this number of projects otherwise. In addition, Canadians are buying second homes in Florida, as the availability of financing from American banks for second homes is starting to loosen up, often requiring down payments ranging from 20 to 35 percent.

It should come as no surprise that most of the buyers of second homes are baby boomers, the majority of whom live in the northeast United States. In addition to having a warmer climate, the cost of living in Florida is less than living in the northern United States—another benefit of moving. If we assume that 20 percent of the 34.5 million boomers living in the northeastern United States start moving south, that would mean 6.9 million people looking for homes. It is clear that the housing supply would not be sufficient to meet that demand and, for the first time for many years, more people would be buying properties in Florida than selling. The population influx that may occur will add to an already densely populated state (Florida is the fourth most populous state)—from 2000 to 2010, Florida's population grew from 16 million to 18.8 million, a rate of 17.6 percent.

Where in Florida?

The possible inward flux of boomers is just one factor in Florida's favor, however. Florida is more than just warm weather, beaches, and golf, in the same way that Orlando is more than just theme parks and Jacksonville is home to more than just the NFL's Jaguars. As one example, Genting, a Malaysian company whose revenues exceed those of Las Vegas, has purchased two sites in Miami and proposes to build a casino plus a 5,300-room hotel and other commercial and retail space. If this proposal is passed, the project will create approximately 100,000 jobs. The state is looking to license five casinos in total. Moreover, Miami has a major international airport, which makes travel to and from the state easier from different parts of the world.

KEY INSIGHT

Florida is more than just a theme park; other parts of the state are worthy of the shrewd investor's attention.

Orlando brought in more than 50 million visitors last year, beating New York City as the most visited city in the country for the first time. A major reason visitors come to Orlando is to see the theme parks at Disney, Epcot, and Universal Studios; however, the reason Orlando is a desirable city in which to live is because it also has a vibrant economy:

- Orlando has a high-tech corridor that employs upwards of 40,000 people.

- It is home to the Central Florida Research Park, the seventh largest research park in the United States, employing 8,500 people.

- It is emerging as a "medical city" with the University of Central Florida (the second largest university in the United States) having a research budget of over $122 million.

Jacksonville, by contrast, is almost a secret despite the fact that it is the largest city in Florida. It is not a tourist destination but is, in many respects, a growing economic engine. Consider that Jacksonville is home to the third largest naval air base in the United States, which employs over 30,000 active-duty personnel and nearly 20,000 civilians. The median age in the city is a young 35.2 years old, and people are earning above-average yearly incomes at $66,791. The private sector has created over 30,000 jobs since the year 2000, and these jobs are driving population growth, which is expected to increase by 3.7 percent by 2016. Why by 2016? Because Jacksonville is one of the first three deep-water ports on the east coast that will be properly equipped to handle the new ships that will come through a newly expanded Panama Canal, due to be completed in 2014.

Tampa is another city in Florida that is very urbanized, but also very close to some of the most popular beaches for foreigners: St Petersburg, Clearwater, and Sarasota. It benefits from a strong local economy that supports three major league sports teams. Tampa has four Fortune 500 companies headquartered in the region and the total worth of all of the companies in the city is more than $19 billion. A lot of growth has been fueled by the over $1.1 billion in venture capital that has been invested since the year 2000, and the medical industry is a massive boon for the Tampa/St Petersburg/Clearwater area. The medical industry is responsible for over 51,000 jobs and over $5 billion in economic activity annually. Annual personal income growth currently sits at 4.3 percent, and employment growth is 2.2 percent annually, which is second highest among all the metropolitan statistical areas. Tampa's *gross metro product* (similar to the GDP of a country) is projected to be the second highest in the state of Florida. The result of the strong economy is population growth of 22 percent from 2000 to 2012, and projections to 2015 show that 60,000 new residents per annum will call Tampa home.

ARIZONA

Arizona has been a vacation and retirement destination for western Canadians for a long time. It's their equivalent of eastern Canada's Florida, due to its warm weather, short flight time, and perpetual golf season. Unlike Florida, Arizona has the added advantage of not suffering hurricanes. During the housing boom, it was one of the most built-up states in all of the United States, and subsequently was one of the hardest hit by the recession. But therein lies the great opportunity for investing and buying a second home in Arizona.

According to CoreLogic, Arizona had one of the highest increases in property values. According to the Zillow Home Value Index, the highest state average price was reached in February 2006 at $265,000, and the lowest in August 2011 at $126,000. As of March 2012, the average home price in the state is recovering and now sits at $130,000. In Phoenix, MLS listings are back to a level considered normal, as are inventory levels, with a 90-day supply.

You can see from the median sale prices below, that the major areas and cities of Arizona have stabilized and are already on the upswing.

City	Peak Median Price	Lowest Median Price	Median Price May 2012
Phoenix	$235k	$80k	$108k
Scottsdale	$467k	$211k	$312k
Mesa	$232k	$101k	$126k
Tempe	$260k	$125k	$159k

As in Florida, Arizona housing prices are rising despite the fact that there are still a lot of underwater mortgages and negativity trickling out of the housing and credit crisis. As per the *CoreLogic Negative Equity Report*, Arizona has a foreclosure inventory of 2.5 percent, a ninety-day-plus delinquency rate of 6.7 percent, and 48.3 percent of mortgaged homes are in negative equity territory.

KEY INSIGHT

Arizona was hard hit by the recession, but is bouncing back.

If you are asking yourself why Arizona is one of the strongest housing markets in the United States, let's consider these key factors: population and economy. Phoenix is the largest state capital in the United States with a population of 1.45 million according to 2010 Census figures. More importantly, from a state-wide perspective, in the period from 2000 to 2010 Arizona's population grew from 5.1 million to 6.4 million, an increase of 24.6 percent.

Arizona does not have land transfer tax, but does charge a state income tax of up to 4.54 percent—still a drop in the bucket compared to what Canadians pay—as well as a rental tax of about 2 percent. The number of housing permits issued in the period from 2000 to 2010 in Arizona was 613,369, a rate of building that is in line with the large population growth. Moreover, when one compares the population increase with the issue of building permits in other states like Florida and New York and Illinois, Arizona's perceived over-building problem is nowhere near as bad as the media makes it seem. It's no wonder that the market is at a healthy level now.

What is even more encouraging is that the unemployment rate in Maricopa County, where Phoenix is located and much of the population of the state lives, is at 7.7 percent, well below the national average, which sits at 8.2 percent at the time of writing this.

TEXAS

Texas is another state that we would highlight because it is the second most populous state in the entire country, has no transfer or income taxes, and has an economy that remained robust throughout and after the recession. Census figures show that the population of Texas increased from 20.9 million to 25.1 million in the period from 2000 to 2010, or by 4.2 million people.

This strong increase in population has also fueled a relatively stable housing market, despite the fact that home prices have yet to rebound. According to Zillow, the high median sale price for the state as a whole was $117,000, reached in July 2007, and the low is $77,000, where it currently hovers. The housing market has not yet rebounded with the same vigor of Florida or Arizona. But considering the large population of the state, and the fact that 1.7 million building permits were issued from 2000 to 2010, the Texas over-supply problem is not nearly as bad as some of the other densely populated states such as New York or Illinois. Here are current median sales price numbers, courtesy of Trulia.

City	Peak Median	Lowest Median Price	Median Price May 2012
Houston	$95k	$55k	$91k
Dallas	$87k	$49k	$64k
Austin	$150k	$50k	$117k
San Antonio	$98k	$52k	$76k

KEY INSIGHT

Texas has great economic fundamentals.

According to CoreLogic, the foreclosure inventory in Texas is 1.4 percent, the ninety-day-plus delinquency rate is 4.9 percent, and negative equity mortgages are at 10.2 percent. By comparing these numbers to those of Florida and Arizona, we can see that Texas is actually in very good economic condition and Texas home prices were up 0.4 percent year over year in February 2012. In fact, Florida, Arizona, and Texas are the only three states that have shown a year-over-year increase in home prices as of February 2012. Compare this to Illinois which has seen a decrease of 7.1 percent; Georgia, which is down 6.6 percent; and California, which is down 3.4 percent.

One thing we have learned from experience is that for the most part, jobs fuel demand for housing. We can see a stabilizing housing market in Texas because the Texas unemployment rate declined to 7.1 percent in February 2012, and the Texas unemployment rate continues to be lower than the US rate. Texas regularly beats the national average for creating jobs, a lot of it fueled by logistics, shipping, and the oil industry.

PART **II**

THE DISTRESSED PROPERTY MARKET

7 Learn to Identify a Distressed Property

Simply defined, a *distressed property* is

> A property where either the physical condition of the property is distressed or the owner of the property is in a financially distressed situation. In some cases, the property and owner are both distressed. The level of distress often motivates decisions to sell and can intensify the potential for price discounts.

At least one of these two factors (physical condition or owner distress) must be in place for a property to be considered a distressed property, and the simultaneous occurrence of both factors definitely increases the odds for a better deal.

WHAT CAUSES DISTRESS

Property owners may not want to deal with a particular property for a variety of personal and financial reasons, causing the property to fall into the distressed properties category. Death and divorce are two of the most obvious reasons.

As we've seen, in recent years, the number one contribution to the growth in the number of distressed properties on the US market is financial hardship, where the owner can no longer afford the property, and in many cases, took on too much financial responsibility when the property was purchased. The owner may have bought at subprime mortgage rates without a plan to reduce debt before the rates rose, or lost employment income during the latest economic recession, or be paying on an underwater mortgage. Regardless of how it happened, the owner is behind on property loan payments.

Once that happens and the properties are in distress, these homes may end up in a *short-sale situation* (where the owner and lender endeavor to sell the property as quickly as possible). Other properties will be *foreclosed* upon, which is when the bank assumes ownership of the property in lieu of missed payments. In either situation, the banks are now in a position of wanting to sell the property.

VOLUME SELLERS SOUTH OF THE BORDER

The fallout of the real estate market correction of 2008 made "foreclosure" the buzzword for distressed property sales south of the 49th parallel. To profit from this situation, you must understand what's really going on in this market.

As we discussed in earlier Insights, you should recognize that right now in the United States, banks are one of the biggest volume sellers of homes. And make no mistake, they are very motivated to sell these homes, often at significantly reduced prices.

To capitalize on those deals, however, Canadian investors need to be able to assess a given market and determine whether the price discount on a particular property is enough to warrant buying it. We will look at the issue of a "bad" versus "good" neighborhood in Insights 12 and 13. For now, understand that if an area has low inventory levels and steady sales at steady prices, you'll have to look harder to find bargain distressed properties. Properties in those areas won't likely be available at a deep discount.

KEY INSIGHT

Aim for facts over hype. Don't neglect your responsibility for market due diligence just because the sign says "Foreclosure."

Given all the media excitement over the foreclosure market, the need to look beyond market hype is one lesson Canadian real estate investors sometimes find difficult to put into action. Let's look at an example: Joe is a successful real estate investor in Virginia Beach, Virginia. He has bought hundreds of properties in his career and he owns a very large rental portfolio in that area. Last year, Joe visited Florida to see some of the properties available in the market there.

He was amazed at the discounts that market-savvy investors were getting. "Fifty cents on the dollar!" he kept saying in disbelief. "Unbelievable! Distressed properties in my area are going for 85 cents on the dollar—even higher!"

The difference between these two markets in the same country intrigued Joe. It turned out that because the Virginia market had remained steadier during the market correction, the level of motivation for distressed sellers was much lower in Virginia Beach versus Florida. Without that motivation to sell, the discounts being offered were not the same.

Florida, on the other hand, had experienced higher foreclosure levels and higher inventory levels and was attracting fewer active buyers. In its purest sense, this was market supply and demand at work!

RESIST THE TEMPTATION TO THINK YOU'RE DIFFERENT

Some investors reading Joe's story will think that maybe Joe just didn't know what he was doing in Virginia Beach. Others might think they can go into a market like Florida and make a good real estate investment having done almost no due diligence.

The truth is that Joe from Virginia Beach is a very good real estate investor and he's on the "inside track" for distressed property sales in his area. If there's a deal in Virginia Beach, Joe knows how to find it and how to get the best discounts available.

He was taken aback by the situation in Florida only because he hadn't yet done his due diligence to see the dramatic differences between those two distressed markets. A deal that costs you 50 cents on the dollar in Florida will almost always need a significant rehab. When you're paying 85 to 90 cents on the dollar in Virginia Beach, that investment won't need a lot of renovation work. (And if it does, you probably paid too much!)

KEY INSIGHT

Canadian real estate investors should know they can go into the American market for distressed property and make money. But it's essential to pay attention to market fundamentals and understand that they differ from state to state, city to city, and neighborhood to neighborhood.

WHAT'S BEHIND THE DISCOUNT?

This brings up another interesting point: Investors who are willing and able to rehab a home that is in a distressed condition really can score some great discounts. And those discounts are especially common in areas where banks have a lot of inventory.

This situation exists because, even with proposed Federal Reserve rules in their December 2011 White Paper allowing banks to hold fore-closed properties on their books, most banks do not want to be in the business of home ownership for the investment market. The banks do not like to own property because that's outside the core competency of their business model, which is to make interest profits off the money they loan out.

That's a problem for banks because, at least for now, banks are the largest seller of distressed property. In fact, distressed property ownership equates to underperforming real estate investments and it greatly affects a bank's lending ability and its overall stock value. The need to improve their lending ability and stock value makes it important for banks to clear out this real estate inventory as quickly and as efficiently as possible. But they also have another concern: banks, like property owners everywhere, have learned that the longer they hold onto underperforming properties, the greater the chance that the condition of the assets will deteriorate even further.

Besides all that, banks as property owners also find themselves on the hook for property taxes and property insurance, meaning the distressed property will cost them real money as long as it's in their portfolio. It remains to be seen whether banks will take advantage of the new rules once (if) they are enacted by the Federal Reserve and hold properties as rental portfolios.

Moreover, bank representatives typically freak out when they see roof damage, plumbing leaks, overgrown front yards, and the like. Why? Because just as banks are not in the business of managing real estate investment property, they're certainly not in the business of renovating homes for resale. The bottom-line message is that when a bank decides how to price the house, its motivation to offer a deep discount peaks if all it has to market that property are ugly pictures of a house in disrepair.

KEY INSIGHT

Understand the bank's motivation to sell distressed property at a discount, especially if the property is physically distressed as well. Recognize, too, that a bank's motivation to discount prices drops as their inventory declines. This is why it's important to look at the US market for distressed properties today, not next year.

SO, THERE'S MONEY TO BE MADE

Part 3 of this book is going to look at the key issues with respect to managing property renovations for the buy-and-flip and buy-and-hold markets. That's a priority because Canadian real estate investors recognize that property rehabs are a proven way to make money in real estate, especially when big discounts are being offered.

Before we get to that, however, let's take a closer look at what this "distressed property" market is all about. You should understand how the American foreclosure system works, as well as some of the other investment fundamentals you need to know if you want to embark on a wealth-building strategy that aims to capitalize on the circumstances at play in the US real estate market.

KEY INSIGHT

The best distressed property deals are in markets that got hit by the downturn, but have positive underlying fundamentals that make them a good long-term market to invest in.

The best deals also require some renovation and repair work, so we recommend that you consider property rehabilitation a critical part of this game.

8

Understand the Fundamentals of the US Foreclosure Process

If you're a Canadian who's been thinking about investing in real estate, you're probably a Canadian who's been thinking about investing in residential home foreclosures south of the 49th parallel. And why not? American residential real estate foreclosures are a hot topic in today's investment circles, and wealth gurus on both sides of the border are asking their students to take a serious look at foreclosed real estate in the United States.

Before you take that step, let's look at how the US foreclosure process works and explore the market basics that make it worth your time and money.

FORECLOSURE DEFINED

Generally speaking, a *US residential real estate foreclosure* involves a situation where a homeowner holds legal title to a property and the bank places a lien or mortgage on the house for the amount owed. The lien remains with the bank/lender; the borrower holds title. In the event of a default on the loan, the bank notifies the borrower and requests that the borrower make up payments. After ninety days, or three missed payments, the bank has the legal right to begin the foreclosure process and take back the house in lieu of missed payments.

Depending on the state, the actual foreclosure can take anywhere from 112 days to two years. In today's economy, the process can take even longer because the banks don't really want to take back more houses. This reluctance to get the property off their books is not a business-as-usual approach to how banks usually sell foreclosed property!

KEY INSIGHT

Foreclosures have always represented an investment opportunity to real estate investors. Some investors in Canada and the United States have specialized in this sector. The current foreclosure market is different because of the number of properties under foreclosure.

The Homeowner's Rights

If you are buying houses that have been foreclosed on in the United States, you should know that the homeowner has some rights. First, the bank cannot take back a house unless one of the following conditions is met: the house goes into a foreclosure auction or the borrower voluntarily deeds the house back to the bank in lieu of a foreclosure. As the foreclosure auction is more common, we focus on that here.

Foreclosure Auction

In a *foreclosure auction*, the bank auctions the house at the local county courthouse for the amount it wishes to receive. If no one bids on the house, or if the opening bid set by the bank is too high for any bidders, the bank gets the house back and lists the property with a local real estate agent. Such properties—those owned by a lender, usually a bank—are placed in a class called *real estate owned (REO)*.

The Big Picture

A great many American homeowners found themselves in tough situations, as housing prices in general fell because people weren't buying houses. Although some markets and the economy overall are showing signs of recovery, let's face it, if people don't have money, they're not buying houses. In what can only be described as a vicious economic cycle, some people may, however, still have to put their houses on the market for any number of reasons, in spite of soft prices.

KEY INSIGHT

From an investor's position, a strong foreclosure market means some homes not in foreclosure will also sell for bargain prices simply because so many of the neighbors have defaulted on their loans. Ahh, supply and demand. Now there's a residential real estate fundamental that matters.

Since numbers tell the story better than any market insider or wealth guru, let's take a look at some US foreclosure stats from 2012. We saw in Insight 1 that from September 2008 to April 2012, there were 3.6 million foreclosures across the United States. According to CoreLogic, the five states with the largest number of completed foreclosures for the twelve months ending in April 2011 were California (142,000), Florida (92,000), Michigan (60,000), Texas (58,000), and Georgia (57,000). These five states account for 48.8 percent of all completed foreclosures nationally. In addition, there are presently 1.6 million more homes in *shadow inventory*—homes that could be foreclosed because they are technically in default.

What the Numbers Really Mean

Taken at face value, those numbers are shocking. But as you will learn in the next Insight about national housing prices, numbers tell only part of the story. Indeed, Insights 12 and 13 on "bad" and "good" neighborhoods will give you some valuable perspective on why some US neighborhoods have weathered the economic downturn and residential housing market corrections much better than others.

In the meantime, remember that the very *worst* state in the entire United States reached a foreclosure high of 3 percent, but is now down to *1.45 percent*. That's still high when compared to the normal historic rates, which sit at less than 1 percent. When Canadians are asked to estimate the rate of foreclosures in states like Nevada, however, they routinely cite figures of 15, 20, and 30 percent. Some go even higher—and those estimates are dead wrong. The actual number in the worst state was 3 percent. Period.

From an investment perspective, that means a lot of American homeowners are still paying their mortgages. And that means that while foreclosures equal investment opportunities, you shouldn't expect to be shooting fish in a barrel! And be aware that according to the US Census Bureau, 32 percent of Americans own their homes without mortgages.

KEY INSIGHT

Do your homework and avoid market hype that gets in the way of sound investment decisions. Residential real estate foreclosures can present great investment opportunities. But the only recipe for success begins and ends with due diligence that includes real market analysis. Always get the facts *before* you act.

9

Commit to the Number One Rule, Then Get Your Options Straight

In this Insight, we'll take a look at the three ways you can go about buying a US property in foreclosure, but first, it is important that you understand the number one rule about foreclosures: **Not every foreclosure is a good deal!**

Commit that rule to memory. Foreclosed real estate properties in the single-family homes market do present investment opportunities and this market is not going away anytime soon. But not every foreclosure is a good deal. Always put your faith in market fundamentals—whether the property you are looking at is in good standing or in foreclosure.

THREE WAYS TO BUY

Now that you've recommitted to taking a good look at the market fundamentals of how a property fits your investment portfolio, let's look at the three stages in which you can go about buying foreclosed properties:

- Short sale
- Auction
- Real estate owned (REO)

Each of the three stages occurs at different times in the foreclosure process. All three have their pros and cons and smart investors will use that information to decide if a particular foreclosure merits their investment cash.

In every case, as an investor, you will want to inspect the home prior to purchase because it is important to know the condition of the house before submitting your offer. In most cases, you will have to repair the home after you purchase. And as a Canadian, remember, you will need to hire American contractors to renovate the home because Canadians cannot work in the United States without a visa.

Short Sale

The first stage is the short sale. Here, the bank agrees to settle for less than what's owed on the loan. In terms of opportunity, this is the first time an outside buyer can get involved with a foreclosure process. At this point, the troubled homeowner is generally behind in his mortgage payments and has put the house on the market with a real estate agent. The asking price is typically less than the amount of the mortgage on the property, so the bank will need to approve the offer. In cases like this, the bank will appoint a *loss mitigator* to handle the file. This is the main point of contact from the bank.

Among the pros of the short sale is that an investor is able to get full access to the property. From a property analysis perspective, this is critical. As well, as the bank is still involved, an investor may be able to get financing for the property versus paying cash. There is also the opportunity for a discounted price and, if the deal proceeds, the buyer will have clean title to the property.

On the negative side, banks in short-sale situations can take a very long time to make a decision. (Loss mitigators are typically buried in files.) Some potential buyers leave the short-sale situation frustrated, feeling they have been strung along for months. In some cases, the loss mitigator may forego your offer and bring the house to auction instead. This is especially frustrating if the bank takes the property to auction at a lower price than your short-sale offer. And yes, that happens, sometimes just because a particular file was lost in the pile of files. This is one area where it's very important that an investor's due diligence includes making sure that a bank's loss mitigator knows who you are and what you're prepared to offer.

Making the Short Sale Work

If you are going to buy in a short sale, make sure the real estate agent involved in the sale rides the loss mitigator hard. This is a situation where the squeaky wheel gets the oil. If you do not stay on top of the file, it might be overlooked.

That usually means that you have to go to a real estate agent and show your willingness to spend several hundred thousand dollars to make a few deals in order to make it worth the agent's time. If you don't have a lot of funds to invest, most experienced realtors in the United States will not work with you on short sales. There is a lot of work involved in closing a deal on a short-sale property and according to insiders, the success rate is only around 12 percent. On top of that, it takes anywhere between two and eighteen months to hear whether the bank is accepting or rejecting the offer. Be prepared to pay a fee rather than commission for the work.

KEY INSIGHT

An experienced realtor who has a track record of getting short sales completed is a plus.

Auction

Stage two of the foreclosure process is the auction sale, where the house can be bought at the court house steps. In this situation, the bank has had enough. It is not accepting short-sale offers and has proceeded with the paperwork to set an auction date for the property at the local county courthouse. This gives an investor the chance to bid on the property and pay cash. The bank sets the opening bid amount.

The number one benefit of the auction scenario is the potential for huge price discounts. As well, you'll leave the auction knowing whether you got the property (no waiting!) and it's possible there will be less competition than at the short-sale stage.

But the disadvantages are real. First, you must pay cash for an auctioned property, usually at the time of the auction or within twenty-four hours. Also, you won't get clear title to the property and there may be serious title issues lurking in the background, including additional liens. You also will have only limited access to the property before the sale, and you may have to deal with a very unhappy resident if anyone still lives in the home.

Making the Auction Work

If you plan to buy at an auction, you need cash and you need to do your homework. You must make sure there are no other liens on the property and that you are bidding on the right mortgage. Once you buy for cash at the auction (also called "buying on the steps"), all sales are final. That means you will inherit any problems with the property.

KEY INSIGHT

Auction sales are a very local game and players are usually full-time local investors who target this niche. Because the due diligence can be intense and mistakes can be costly, respect that auctions are serious business.

Real Estate Owned

At this third stage of a foreclosure, the home has gone through the auction process and there were no bidders, so the bank has the property back. The property is assigned to an asset manager at the bank and that person hires a local real estate agent to list the property for sale the same way other properties are listed. This is now called a bank real estate owned (bank REO) property. It is considered a bad debt on the bank's balance sheet, so the lender wants to get rid of it.

Real estate agents working in the REO field can have some great deals, and working with these agents can be very rewarding. Always remember that banks prefer cash and they usually want to close an REO deal quickly to get the bad debt off their books. (They also do not want to be in the property management business, as we discussed in Insight 7.)

On the plus side, REOs offer large discount potential. With a real estate agent involved, investors can get full access to the property. As an added bonus, REO property is vacant, so investors do not have to deal with the emotions of the people living in that house. Buyers also will get clear title and the entire process is much faster and more predictable than the short-sale process. Investors who like doing business in the REO stage of the distressed property market may access repeat business if they have good relationships with high-volume REO real estate agents.

The quick close and the fact that you usually have to pay cash for the property are two key disadvantages of the REO. As well, there tends to be more competition for these homes.

Making the REO Work

You can make money here—in fact, some investors focus on the REO niche market—but you need to research and track the REO listings constantly. You also need to build a good working rapport with an REO agent. Again, as with the short sales, most experienced US realtors will not work with investors unless they have a lot of funds to invest. The long time it takes to make offers is often prohibitive to the process.

KEY INSIGHT

This is one niche where relationships really matter. If you can't keep current with REO listings, you'll need to find someone who can. You also need to know agents who target this market.

WHAT TO REMEMBER ABOUT FORECLOSURES

Foreclosures are a great niche market for real estate investment deals. But not every foreclosure is a good deal. There are investors who are willing to sacrifice due diligence and solid fundamentals just because the property is called a "foreclosure." The main point is that you need to cut through the media hype when it comes to overplayed terms like "foreclosure." Here's what you really need to know:

- A foreclosure is a house that is owned by a bank.

- A bank, just like other distressed sellers, will sometimes list their homes for a high sale price hoping that someone will bite. This can happen at the short-sale, auction, or REO stages of the foreclosure process.

- Each stage of the process has different pros and cons.

- Investors can and do pay more than they should for foreclosed properties.

- Investors can and do end up with major rehab headaches when they buy foreclosed properties without seeing them first, or before they've done any real property analysis.

- The best offence is a great defence. Know your numbers and have a clear strategy that you can execute to make money with the property.

- You can nibble, but don't bite until you've done your homework.

FOREWARNED IS FOREARMED

Three things can happen when a Canadian investor starts looking at the US foreclosure market. Some investors will make money. Others will lose money. Members of the third group will throw up their hands in despair and leave the market when it turns out that every foreclosure is not a great deal.

One sage investor says that to avoid giving up too early, market newcomers should know three things:

- If you look at ten houses, five will be dogs and priced too high.

- If you look at ten houses, three will be "okay" deals, but not "great" deals.

- If you look at ten houses, two will be really good and absolutely worth your time and effort.

When he finally finds a house with potential, this investor likely will make an offer—and it will be less than what the bank is asking for. Remember: the bank is a distressed seller!

10

More on Due Diligence

As a real estate investor, you want the best information you can find regarding investment opportunities. In other words, you need market-specific information to help you calculate the potential for a particular property. Without that relevant data, your choices lack direction.

In 2009, for example, residential real estate markets in Stockton, California, experienced one of the steepest drops in value across the United States. Those numbers may be statistically in line with what happened at the national level; however, a closer look shows neighboring cities a few hours west of Stockton experienced healthy growth throughout the entire market correction. While national housing statistics would lead you to conclude that *every* market in the United States has discounted properties for sale because *every* market in the United States lost value in the last crash, this example illustrates how that is absolutely not the case!

By the same token, an oversupply of houses in certain areas of Phoenix, Arizona, does not necessarily have any impact on an investor's attempts to fill rental properties with tenants in Jacksonville, Florida. The fact that property values in Miami dropped almost 50 percent also does not translate into a scenario where you can buy a house for fifty cents on the dollar in San Francisco.

What's going on? The fundamentals for each market are totally different. Not every market underwent a huge correction and, therefore, some markets will not have the huge discounted property sales that you read about in the paper. Moreover, even when a particular market experiences a significant correction, the fact that "cheap" properties are on the market does not guarantee that market is a good place to invest.

Look at your own city and your own neighborhood. Market variances are a fact of life in every real estate market. As an investor, you need to know how to figure out what the numbers *mean*. It's your job to get past the "fluff" and pay attention to what really matters. The media will bombard us with statistics, but we can still keep our eyes on the prize! That's where the Property Goldmine Scorecard from Insight 2 becomes useful—by focusing on the stats that matter.

FIVE MARKET FUNDAMENTALS

There are five fundamentals that drive individual real estate markets:

- Economic growth
- Population growth
- Affordability
- Desirability
- Supply and demand

These fundamentals are a fantastic guide to what really matters when choosing the right market in which to invest. Remember: information is power and once you commit to these fundamentals, your investment strategy will be powered by information that matters.

KEY INSIGHT

When you are assessing the investment potential of real estate property, aim for five out of five and never be satisfied with anything less than four!

Economic Growth

Zero in on the local economy and find data for local economic indicators of

- Job activity/employment
- New company growth
- Military growth

- Various economic resources
  - Is the area dependent on one industry or job source?
  - Are there opportunities to buy rentals close to an important job source? (The farther you are from a significant employer, the more troubled the market during an economic downturn.)

Population Growth

What is the local population doing in terms of growth? Certain US markets have been shown to be shrinking in population at a steady pace. Other markets are growing and predicted to continue growing for years to come.

Much of that predicted growth is due to baby boomers retiring and deciding to spend their money in warm climate states like Florida, Arizona, Nevada, and California. Several of the areas popular with baby boomers were hit hard in the market correction. What's that noise? Sounds like opportunity knocking! But think about those 34.5 million baby boomers living in the northern United States. How many of them want to stop shoveling snow when they retire, and move to the sunnier climates of the south, where the cost of living is also cheaper? What percentage do you think will be moving? If you assume that 30 percent decide to move, that's 10.4 million people. The supply of housing isn't there, meaning that the prices for those that do exist will improve. The message? Don't wait. Buy now.

Affordability

The lack of affordability is a big cause of the recent downturn in certain markets. But some of the markets with the most "affordable" housing also have shrinking populations, no jobs and, by default, not much opportunity for real estate investors.

Desirability

Real estate investors are not buying properties they will live in. They are buying properties others will want to live in. Always be realistic about what a property offers a renter in that market.

- What is close to the property? Airports, transportation for easy commuting?

- Why would someone want to live there?

- What does it offer in terms of lifestyle, warm weather, and proximity to amenities (groceries, recreation, sports, and the arts)?

Supply and Demand

During the economic boom of the mid 2000s, some American cities were overbuilt. There were not enough people to fill all of the houses that were being built, even when the economy was firing on all cylinders. Other areas experienced significant devaluation when populations were depleted by job losses.

Your goal is to enter a market that has a positive balance of supply and demand, or is moving in that direction because of economic and population growth alongside factors like affordability and desirability.

The need to consider all market fundamentals has never been more important. Industry insiders, for example, consider Las Vegas to be an overbuilt market. But investors who turn their backs on that market, based on the supply and demand market fundamental, may be missing the rest of the Las Vegas story. While inventory may be high, this city's resale volume has hit record highs and the inventory is dropping.

Also be sure to investigate what type of property has high vacancy rates in the area you are researching. In some areas, condos are in oversupply but single-family homes priced below the median value are in undersupply.

AN EXTRA WORD ON VACANCY RATES

Vacancy rates also hold a wealth of important information for real estate investors who are trying to determine the potential of a market. This information is typically available from a quality real estate agent or property manager. But always go beyond the surface data. Real estate agents and property managers do not have a vested interest in your ability to make money, but rather a vested interest in their own business goals.

If you learn that the vacancy rate in a particular market looks pretty good from an investment perspective, you need to take that information and look at what's behind the numbers. Find out what kinds of properties people are renting. Are there areas where it is tougher to find renters? We can see areas where the market vacancy rate has been pegged at more than 10 percent, but some property managers will report that their properties run at about 2 to 5 percent. This probably speaks to high demand for the type of property they own and a practical commitment to excellent property management.

KEY INSIGHT

Once you know the vacancy rates, review the five market fundamentals to see what else they can tell you about a residential real estate market's investment potential. If a quality tenant has several properties to choose from, what kind of property is he or she most apt to select? What can you do to make your property number one?

MORE MARKET FACTS

Market fundamentals are critical to your assessment of a market, but they don't tell you anything about a particular property's investment potential. Here, we recommend that real estate investors calculate one more figure into their decision-making toolkit: the 1-percent marker.

The 1-Percent Marker

Once you know that the market fundamentals tell you a real estate market deserves a closer look, you need to go looking for what successful investors call the 1-percent marker. This is a simple and effective way to assess a potential deal. Here's how it works:

> **Using the purchase price and cost of initial repairs,**
> **look for a 1-percent gross a month in rent.**

Say you bought a house for $100,000 and it's ready to rent. Rent is $1,000 a month, which equals 1 percent of the purchase price. That's good. Similarly, if you buy a house for $90,000 and allocate $10,000 for repairs to get it rent ready, at $1,000 a month for rent, this deal still meets the 1-percent marker rule. That changes for both scenarios as soon as the rent drops below $1,000. The 1-percent marker is equivalent to 12 percent of the purchase price. Compare this to residential investments in Canada where investors typically look for 8 to 10 percent of the purchase price.

What can you tell from the 1-percent marker? As long as your property is subject to fair taxes and insurance, a 1-percent marker means you can cash flow a property. It can be difficult to find a property that hits the five fundamentals and the 1-percent marker, but never turn your back on what the 1-percent marker is telling you.

11

Avoid the Snake-Oil Salesman

It would be nice to write a real estate investment book and never talk about the risk of fraud, but doing so would be impractical. While there is no guarantee that you won't encounter the proverbial snake-oil salesman in Canadian real estate deals, you must be especially wary of fraudsters when working in another country, including one as geographically and culturally close to Canada as the United States.

From this perspective, seminar fakes, lender scams, and housing rip-offs are three subject areas that merit special attention. All three are alive and well in the United States, and all three could present a serious danger to your investing efforts. If you know how to identify them, however, you can avoid them and their ill effects.

When it comes to dealing with people and money, there is no room for complacency regarding fraud. So while we can't explore every aspect of fraud here, we encourage you to be vigilant and to pay keen attention to some of the most powerful warning signs we've learned about.

THERE'S NO SUCH THING AS 'LEADING' OR 'ONLY' EXPERTS

This is one area that few real estate investment insiders want to talk about. But savvy investors who want to create long-term wealth need help standing up to what we'll call the 800-pound gorillas that are ruining the wealth-creation industry.

Paying for specialized knowledge can be one of the best investment decisions you'll ever make—as long as you take the information you've paid for and put it into action. That is, if you get the information you've paid for.

Believe it or not, some of the real estate seminar industry's most popular experts have never bought a property or done investment business in the areas where their seminars are offered. These are professional marketers, not professional investors, and they grab onto popular theories and techniques to position themselves as experts in real estate solely because they can make money at it.

The big problem with these gurus is that because they haven't done deals, they can't possibly know what you need to understand to do those deals. Unfortunately, their pitch is sometimes so good that investors leave their seminars thinking they have valuable information. That enthusiasm quickly deflates when they try to put their new knowledge into practice and realize that without specific investment strategies, they are woefully unprepared to take action (and their wallets are a lot lighter!).

KEY INSIGHT

Some hucksters are really good at convincing seminar-goers that they know what they're talking about. But if they haven't done what they're teaching, they cannot offer insight into how you can avoid the mistakes and pitfalls they've encountered. Some try to give the impression that it's so easy they've never made mistakes. But we'll be brutally honest with you here: every investor makes mistakes. And speakers who can share their tales from the trenches have the most to offer.

So how do you find the right seminar teacher? Here are three points to keep in mind:

Always Go for Real-World Experience

The best seminar teachers are real people. They are down-to-earth, authentic, and straightforward. They teach from personal experience and what they talk about onstage has substance. They speak with sincerity versus taking a sales-pitch approach. They do not brag about material riches, but teach from their success and failures. They are also quick to give credit to those who have helped them along the way.

KEY INSIGHT

The best seminar speakers talk from personal experience. They can answer your questions forthrightly—or willingly point you in the direction of someone who can.

Be on your guard for arrogant seminar speakers. If they know everything, have had nothing but success, and did it all on their own thanks to a superior intellect and fancy techniques, don't be impressed. They're not likely giving you anything of value. A less politically correct description is they are full of you-know-what!

One of the ways to detect that you are going to a seminar sale as opposed to investing in real estate is to look at their marketing material to see if they are talking about tenanted properties that they say can be acquired for $20,000. If you are looking to buy $10,000 and $20,000 properties (yes, they do exist), they normally require a lot of repairs, which as a Canadian, you are not permitted to complete because you require a visa to do the work. On top of that, the chances of purchasing a home for $20,000 in even a remotely decent area are minuscule.

KEY INSIGHT

Gurus put their pants on one leg at a time—just like the rest of us—but some industry "experts" are nothing of the sort. They will take your money without remorse and take no responsibility for the poor quality of the program they've offered.

Value the Easy-to-Understand Explanation

Real estate investment is not rocket science. Be wary of seminar speakers who make the subject confusing. They want you to think you don't "get it." That's essential to their sales pitch: if you stick with me and keep buying my programs and seminars, you'll understand (wink, wink!). Seminars that are all about the newest sales pitch often try to convince investors they have some fancy "system" that is the secret way to huge profits, guaranteed (by the way, there's no such word in real estate investing). These seminar leaders simply love complexity and encourage you to think that's the way it has to be (at least until you understand what they are talking about).

Be suspicious of speakers who talk around a subject when people (also known as paying customers) ask questions.

Look for Content

Content matters, and if you're paying for the information, it really matters. Remember that content is not something you can measure by the size of the seminar binder. Good content is real and practical insights, tools, and street-smart information that you can put to work in your own investment business.

You don't want to pay to hear inflated success stories with very little detail, or pay to listen to sales pitches that always involve buying a bigger, more expensive program with the promise of "bonus" content. If you go to a seminar and the speaker delivers nothing but a sales pitch, expect the same thing from their other programs—and back out of the room with haste.

These are the "carrot-on-the-stick" gurus. They may offer tidbits of valuable information, but you will pay dearly with time and money. These seminar leaders will take a subject that can be taught in one or two sessions and make it a ten-session event. They will make you believe that real estate investing is fraught with complications and only those who sign up for every one of their programs will be successful.

There are groups recruiting the public to come to seminars. The reason they are recruiting is not to sell properties, but to fuel their real business, which is selling seminars. The way it works is that people are invited to attend a public event, where they are invited to attend another seminar where they may pay $1,000 or more. At that seminar, they are then sold another seminar for $5,000. Then they are invited to attend a year-long course that may cost up to $35,000. There are also "mentoring programs" where the annual fees can be $100,000. And the sales pitch isn't only for more seminars. If someone is telling you that you need a fancy phone system, special software programs, websites, expensive marketing, huge letter campaigns and the like just to get started in foreclosures, run away!

KEY INSIGHT

A little education can go a long way. The foreclosure market is attracting a lot of attention amongst financial educators. That popularity attracts sharks. Be prepared to ask the tough questions. Be prepared to expect substance for your cash. Be prepared to do the research to find the seminar that's right for you.

LENDER SCAMS

Getting people to lend you money to make real estate deals happen can be essential to your success. But be careful where you get your money. Here are three of the main things to watch for when it comes to protecting yourself from common lending scams.

Be Wary of Up-Front Requests for Money

If anyone asks you for money up front as a prerequisite to finding you money for your deals, they're not legitimate. No one who can honestly access funds for your real estate deals will need to be paid up front to "find" the money.

This is a very old scam and it plagues the world of private financing. If you're one of the many international investors who turn to the private financing market, remember this warning!

Get a Good Faith Estimate

A *good faith estimate (GFE)* is provided to you by your lender and will put in writing all rates and terms. By having these details in writing, you can avoid the "bait and switch" lender scam. This fraudster will try and trick you into a higher-interest loan or into terms different from those in your verbal agreement. Getting a GFE in writing may not guarantee the rate, but it will help keep the lender honest.

Read Your Loan Documents and Ask Questions

Never sign anything you don't understand. When you work with knowledge-able and experienced advisors, you can call on them for advice you can trust.

HOUSING RIP-OFFS

Housing rip-offs are a scourge on the US real estate market these days, and international investors, including Canadians, are among those at greatest risk. Indeed, international buyers are the ultimate target of the housing rip-off artist.

Most of these scams look pretty much the same. Every aspect of these deals will be promoted based on one main theme: the property is cheap with high cash flow.

In a common application of the housing rip-off, you'll be offered a house for $10,000 to $30,000 with great rent rates. No wonder investors are interested! But if you scratch below the surface of this deal, you typically see that the plan is a house of cards. More specifically, most of the homes are located in cities with terrible fundamentals. That is, the potentially positive indicators you could get from population, economic, desirability of location, and supply and demand data are all pointing in the negative direction. In the end, affordability is the only positive indicator.

Insight 8 looked at the market fundamentals of the foreclosure process. It emphasized the fact that where other market fundamentals are lacking, affordability is an investment deal-breaker. This is especially true if these homes are in terrible areas and/or in terrible condition.

KEY INSIGHT

Housing rip-offs often are promoted by "house groups." They claim to have a plan to renovate entire neighborhoods. Again, do your due diligence. These groups usually do not have an experienced and professional reno crew, nor are they backed by tested and proven management. This is a good way to lose your investment, fast.

Beyond a price that might knock your socks off, these investment scams often employ similar language. For example, they typically claim to involve the ever-so-sexy "bulk deal." Other times, they allude to their special connections with banks as the reason they are able to access homes at such great prices.

Once you look into the property, ideally after you've reviewed the fundamentals, you'll see that while anyone could buy these homes, very few people would ever want them. Vacancies are high, tenant turnover is high, repairs and maintenance are through the roof, management is tough to find, and the area lacks resales.

Some of these scam artists will try to convince you that what makes these deals special is their location in a "great transition neighborhood." Again, put your fundamentals to work. History tells us that when economic times are bad, the quality of life in a bad neighborhood will only get worse.

Another good indicator of a housing rip-off scam is that the group trying to convince you to buy the houses located in questionable areas will not have any of its own money invested there! The group's goal is to collect the money and head for the hills. One of the most frustrating angles to this scam is the fact that when things go wrong, no one from this housing group will be available to take your call. This is in stark contrast to the beginning of the deal, when you will find them always available, promising the sun and the moon.

Look into any claims of what might make a bad neighborhood turn around. Be suspicious. If you can't back up the claims, don't believe them.

KEY INSIGHT

The people behind the housing rip-off scam are not trying to sell you a house because they think it's a good deal. They just know it's easier to find several potential investors with $10,000 than to find one with $90,000. Because their buyers can pay cash at such a low price point, the crooks can be in and out of a neighborhood at top speed. Their goal is to sell more houses, not better houses. Fall prey to this scam and you'll be in a neighborhood of inexperienced investors, all of whom now own the wrong house in the wrong neighborhood.

The Sure Signs of a Housing Rip-Off

Anyone who's spent any time in the American foreclosure market knows that housing rip-off scams are out there—and avoidable. Here's what you need to be on the lookout for when a house group is trying to reel you and your money into the wrong property:

- The cheap price is all they promote. The deal focuses on affordability. This way, the investors typically won't need to finance the deal and the scammer can easily skip town with the money.

- They promise high rent returns. Estimated rents are just a theory, so do your homework. These properties tend to be located in areas with above-average vacancy rates, higher repair averages, higher tenant turnovers, and higher damage claims. Once you do the math, you'll know that the promise of extra cash flow is all smoke and mirrors. This property isn't going to make you money—it's going to cost you money.

- The homes are always run down and located in bad neighborhoods. They are always marketed as affordable fixer-uppers in "transition neighborhoods." If there's high crime, high vacancy, no first-time home-buyers, and a wealth of investor-owned property, then the neighborhood is a long way from transitioning towards gentrification.

- The sales pitch will claim the house needs very little work to become "rent ready." That's often code for "the home is so run down that it's uninsurable."

- The people behind the deal talk big numbers: "We buy twenty, thirty, fifty houses a month." The smart investor knows to ask if that's a good thing. If you're buying fifty homes a month, you're renovating fifty homes a month. You're also looking for fifty good tenants a month. Without some major support, these numbers spell nothing but trouble. When the area implodes, investors will left holding the pieces.

KEY INSIGHT

Housing rip-off scams leave a lot of international real estate investors in their wake. Market-wise investors know that greed is a bad source of motivation. When a deal looks too good to be true, it probably is.

- The investors talk about how they are investing in several markets. Again, that's not always a good thing. Canadian investors looking at the US market should proceed with caution and focus on one market, at least until they gain some real-world experience. Good investors know they need to pay attention to ensure their business strategies work. If the people you are dealing with are in ten different markets, then they need ten different teams on the ground and every one of those teams must be able to perform. Think about how complicated it would be to put that together. Now use that skepticism to avoid getting taken in.

- The investors claim they have rent-to-own tenants ready to go and buyers basically lining up to buy you out of the property within a few years. They also will tell you they can get a "government Section 8 tenant" to move in. (Rent is subsidized for Section 8 tenants.)

What they won't tell you is that tenants who qualify for assistance through the US Department of Housing and Urban Development (HUD) have lots of choices about where they live. Remember what happens to a bad neighborhood in an economic downturn? It gets worse. People will always move to a better area when that choice is available. And in today's US market, it's available.

- The house group selling these homes will not own any property in the area.

- The house group can talk the talk, but never walks the walk. The house group will not have a track record. Since market fundamentals are all about the track record, this is a problem.

Questions to Ask

As part of your due diligence, it makes sense to ask a few questions when you come across a great deal. The answers to these questions will help you identify a housing rip-off:

- How long have you been investing in the area?

- Do you have rental property in the area?

- How do you handle property management?

- Where do you find your contractors? Have they been tested?

- Can I look at some testimonials and client references for your property managers and contractors?

Other real estate investors can help you make money. You should not let them help you lose money. Never confuse "affordability" with a deal that's too good to pass up.

12 Recognize That a Bad Area in the United States Is Very Different from a Bad Area Elsewhere

You're likely not familiar with every city in Canada. But you would learn more about a given city if you were going to invest there. In the same way, Canadians doing business in the United States should bone up on what makes some cities, or parts of those cities, remarkably different from their Canadian counterparts. Guess what? It's got to do with more than the weather!

There is an old story about two tourists heading to the zoo in New York that illustrates this point beautifully. It seems the tourists got off at the wrong station and were spotted by a police officer doing patrol. When asked what they were looking for they replied, "The zoo." The police officer looked at them and said, "You're in it. Now get the hell out of here."

DEFINE YOUR BAD AREA

The most important point for investors to understand is that a "bad" area in a US city is very different from a "bad" area in a Canadian city. Canadian real estate investors ignore this at their peril.

There is another story about an American investment advisor who once got to tour some Canadian cities with a good friend who was also a very successful real estate investor with an impressive portfolio. As they drove around and looked at properties, they came to a neighborhood where the Canadian owned several investments. The Canadian warned his American friend that they were entering "the dangerous part of the city." He wasn't trying to be dramatic, he just wanted to give his US colleague a kind of heads up about the community they were about to enter.

The American acknowledged the comment and their conversation returned to a discussion of what was happening in that city's overall real estate market. After a few more minutes passed, the American broke the stride of the conversation and asked, "Hey, when are we going to the bad area of town?" His friend looked at him in disbelief, saying they were in the midst of the bad neighborhood. "Can't you tell?"

This story illustrates a primary difference between the American and Canadian cultural experience. "It wasn't even close to what I expected when he told me we were going to the 'worst' part of the city," said the American.

The tremendous discrepancy in their understandings of what constitutes a bad neighborhood comes from the fact that the two men hailed from radically different environments. Whereas the Canadian investor grew up in Calgary, Alberta, the American investor grew up 30 minutes outside of New York City. The worst Calgary neighborhood was nothing like a bad neighborhood in many of the US cities the American knew. Not even close.

This experience probably holds true for most Canadians and Americans. The basic truth is that a bad neighborhood in the United States is much worse than what most Canadians are accustomed to. In fact, if Canadians going south think that a bad neighborhood in a Canadian city matches a bad neighborhood in the United States, they're in for a nasty wake-up call.

BE REALISTIC

Canadians who are thinking about doing business in the United States need to know they will have to do some basic research about specific markets. That basic research should shed light on some of the fundamental differences in demographics that affect the quality of life in a neighborhood. The raw population data is striking in and of itself. Whereas Canada has some 35 million citizens, the US population hovers at around 325 million.

Population differences aside, there is little to be gained from debating the various reasons for demographic differences in American versus Canadian rates of crime, poverty, etc. In fact, Canadians who want to invest in US real estate should steer clear of talk about gun laws, drug legalization, racial stress, and political parties. You are investing in real estate, not transforming the American political and socio-economic system.

KNOW WHAT YOU NEED TO KNOW

Canadian real estate investors need to be able to identify the right US single-family home neighborhoods in which to invest. This is especially critical when you are investing with others. While some people may be willing to invest in a bad neighborhood in the United States, we would recommend against it. To really protect yourself, you need to make decisions about what constitutes a bad investment neighborhood for you.

For example, an American real estate investment specialist says that in Jacksonville, Florida, he refuses to invest with partners in a neighborhood that is owned solely by landlords or has a strong history of drugs, prostitution, and violence. Period. That rule works for him and keeps his investors happy. In fairness, this same specialist has tried to make a go of "all investor" landlord-owned neighborhoods before, but once burned, twice shy. He now knows that first-time homebuyers can stabilize a market. Where first-time homeowners are absent, the market is more susceptible to a crash. (For more on how this works, read Insight 13.)

WEIGH RISKS AND RETURNS

Canadians who do not understand the incredible differences between a bad neighborhood in Canada and one in the United States should take a closer look at what happened in Jacksonville during the economic boom pre-2008. At that time, investment properties were selling for $140,000 to $145,000. After the most recent correction, these same properties were selling for $20,000 less.

Something entirely different happened in communities populated solely by investor-landlords. In the boom times, homes in these tougher neighborhoods were selling for $80,000 to $85,000. At the time, these homes were considered cheap. After the correction, these same properties sold for $10,000 to $15,000.

Canadian investors who want to understand the US market and the peculiarities of the bad neighborhood must look at what was behind such a drastic change. Fundamentally speaking, investors fled these lower-priced markets during the downturn. They also stopped buying properties in these markets. With more homes on the market and no buyers wanting to purchase them, property values went into a freefall.

Now, guess who really got hurt on these deals. For the most part, it was uneducated out-of-town investors. Not realizing the key market demographics at work, they had bought houses in terrible condition, located in dangerous neighborhoods where no one really wanted to live, and where there was no workable strategy for market improvement (where gentrification was a dream, not a plan). These investors bought into the notion that there was a lot of money to be made thanks to cheap prices and high cash flow. Unfortunately (and unbelievably) they never saw the fundamental flaw in an approach that ignored a key economic reality of the investment market: your property must be located in an area where people want to live.

KEY INSIGHT

Market-savvy Canadian real estate investors must commit and re-commit to understanding the market in which they want to invest.

Want to hear an even sadder investment story? What happened in this segment of the housing market in Jacksonville, Florida, also occurred again and again across the United States in markets that were similarly dominated by landlords. Real estate investors from across the United States and around the world were attracted to the action and a lot of them jumped right in. The smartest investors did not, because they knew these markets had a fundamental flaw. They watched other investors make highly emotional decisions based on low housing prices, but wisely refused to follow the lead of these uninformed investors.

Please take the information in this fundamental as a warning. Canadians investing in US real estate can and should appreciate that there are a lot of cultural similarities between the two countries, but not everything is the same. Once you cross that border, even words like "good neighborhood" and "bad neighborhood" merit closer scrutiny.

TEN WARNING SIGNS OF A BAD NEIGHBORHOOD IN THE UNITED STATES

If you're not sure whether a neighborhood is good or bad from an investment perspective, add this checklist to your due diligence process and do a little independent fact-checking. If several points on the following list hold true, you should probably back away from the neighborhood, and then run!

- Property management is hard to find.

- Good tenants are hard to find.

- There is a high rate of tenant turnover and an even higher vacancy rate.

- Investors report higher maintenance and repair bills compared to other neighborhoods.

- The neighborhood can be dangerous to visit for property checks, maintenance, and repairs, with reports of high crime and violence.

- When comparing changes to property values, prices in this neighborhood dropped faster and farther than in adjacent, "better" neighborhoods.

- The insurance broker quotes higher insurance rates and/or securing adequate insurance is difficult because of the address.

- A check of resale values show prices on the decline.

- Urban crime statistics show higher rates of problems related to drugs, prostitution, and violent crimes.

- More investor scam deals are performed in these neighborhoods.

13

Look for the Stability of a Good Neighborhood and Follow First-Time Homebuyers

Now that you have a sense of why Canadian real estate investors need to avoid bad neighborhoods in the United States, you should know why a combination of homeowners and renters makes for a better investment neighborhood.

First and foremost, look at the facts. Quality market research shows that the problems plaguing investor-landlord communities in the United States are largely absent in neighborhoods where first-time homebuyers are purchasing homes. And this isn't only happening in the good times. Throughout the recent market correction, as prices plummeted in neighborhoods that were dominated by renters, neighborhoods that were attracting a number of first-time homebuyers were characterized by more stable housing prices.

This happened (and will continue to happen) because first-time homebuyers are concerned with terms and condition, not price. This simple fact keeps sales comparably stronger in areas that are attractive to first-time buyers. For this reason alone, we recommend that investors deliberately look for neighborhoods that have a mixture of homeowners and renters.

THE BENEFITS OF MARKET STABILITY

Market stability affects more than housing prices. Having a mix of home-owners and renters in a neighborhood also tends to have a positive influence on property management. Since the people who want to live in these neighborhoods are less transient, they are more likely to take care of the properties they inhabit. Tenants in these neighborhoods also tend to want to own the house they are renting. This is rarely the case in the more troubled areas.

You may be wondering why so many investors continue to look at unstable housing markets as a major opportunity and ignore the real risks involved with investing in them. Basically, it comes down to the difference between investing with facts and investing with wishes.

So, when people say, "I've got $80,000 to invest in the US market and I think I am better off buying four $20,000-houses than I am buying one $80,000-house," we resist the temptation to tell them they're dead wrong, and give a more diplomatic response:

> *"Maybe. But let me ask you this. If someone you know has a horse manure sandwich and they cut it up into little pieces to make it taste better, is that what happens? Does it taste better because they want it to taste better? Or does it still taste like horse manure?"*

Always think your investment strategy through from start to finish. It's true that in the current market you can buy a house in Detroit for $10,000 or less. But some areas have up to *50 percent* (no, that is not a typo) unemployment.

Again, it's all about facts versus wishes.

WHAT'S YOUR INVESTMENT PLAN?

There are investors in the United States who make almost all of their real estate investment money in neighborhoods dominated by landlords and renters. But rest assured these investors are a very particular breed.

First, often they are extremely seasoned investors. They are not guessing what might work in a particular neighborhood; they know. Second, they also live full time in the city where they are investing in these tougher neighborhoods. This gives them constant access to the property and how it's managed. These investors also tend to invest in a large volume of these homes and deliberately stay very involved in day-to-day property management. Where they are not involved in the day-to-day management, they have very strong relationships with quality management and repair services. If this all sounds easy, you're not listening. Here are three things to think about. Canadian real estate investors

- Do not typically know what these neighborhoods are really like, because they are substantially worse than their Canadian counterparts.

- Do not live in the cities where these neighborhoods exist (and may not even want to visit very often).

- Probably do not want to buy large volumes of these properties or be highly involved with their day-to-day management.

KEY INSIGHT

Investors who enter "tough" markets must know exactly what they're getting into. They also must make these investments with proven management already in place so these houses stay rented to paying tenants and repairs are kept under control.

A FINAL WORD OF CAUTION

Why are we so adamant that Canadian real estate investors understand how bad neighborhoods can affect their portfolios? Too many international investors get in over their heads when they buy the wrong house based on the largely emotional attraction of a cheap price. To reiterate the points made in the Insight 12, your dreams of a high-rent return are seriously compromised in neighborhoods with high crime, high tenant turnover, high repairs, and terrible resale prospects. To make things worse, these deals often are made by shyster salespeople who won't return your calls after you buy one of their nightmare properties.

To identify a shyster pitch, look for what's behind a salesperson's use of words like "transitional neighborhoods" or "gentrification." Both are supposed to mean neighborhoods moving towards improvement during good economic times. But in the current market, there are good deals to be had in good neighborhoods that do not need gentrification—they are already good neighborhoods.

Of course, some people who buy property in a bad neighborhood will make money, but the odds are against you. As the great Warren Buffett says, "Price is what you pay, value is what you get."

KEY INSIGHT

One US real estate investor says that he only buys investment properties in neighborhoods that he can walk in at 10 p.m. on a Friday or Saturday and not feel afraid. The fear-free walk cannot be your only point of due diligence, but it is the kind of no-nonsense advice investors should put to work when they're assessing the value of a particular property in a particular neighborhood.

Insight 12 gave you ten items for your bad-neighborhood watch list. Here are a few things you can do when trying to weed out bad neighborhoods and select good ones:

- Visit your investment market.

- Drive through the neighborhoods at different times of the day or night.

- Check local crime statistics.

- Search local newspapers for neighborhood names.

- Spend some time talking to local real estate professionals including real estate agents and property managers.

- Focus on neighborhoods where there are both renters and homeowners.

14

Choose Your Exit Strategy Before You Make the Deal

Two things are very clear in the current US market: first, anyone can buy at a discount, and second, it's what you do after you've made the deal that really matters.

The need to have a solid exit strategy in place as you make an investment deal is old news to experienced investors. They plan to make money when they buy and they know that a deal is defined by its *exit strategy*— their plan for how and when they will sell the investment and take their profit. If you do not have an effective exit strategy in place for the property, you stand to lose money, even if you acquired the property for pennies on the dollar.

That prediction takes a lot of new investors by surprise, so be clear about how important an exit strategy is. In a market like this, it's very easy to get caught up in the deal and not think through the process. That is an abdication of solid due diligence. To drive this fundamental home, we'll share a story based on dozens of phone calls a US investor colleague has fielded in recent months. He's been buying distressed investment properties for years and he says all the calls go like this:

"Hi there! It's me, your newbie investor friend, and guess what? You were totally right about what's going on in the US market for distressed property! I just bought an incredible deal at a huge discount. It was a foreclosure sale and the price was incredible. The single-family home is located in the kind of neighborhood you told me to look at and while it's got a few cosmetic issues I'll need to clear up, it's structurally sound. The HVAC, roof, plumbing, and electrical systems are in great condition,* too, so I figured I've saved some real money there."

"That's wonderful news. What are you going to do with it?"

"Do with it? I'm going to renovate first and then . . ."

* See Insight 24: Do the Big Four Renos on a Rental Property—Now.

The phone goes quiet at this point. After a few moments of awkward silence, some novice investors will insist a plan doesn't really matter "since I got the property so cheap!" Others will dismiss the question as an issue they'll deal with as work proceeds on the property upgrade. Some will stumble with a response as they start to appreciate the magnitude of the question they've just been asked. All three reactions indicate a problem, but at least the last caller is starting to see the forest for the trees.

It does not matter if you're buying real estate investment property in your own backyard or in a foreign country—you need to have an exit strategy. If you cannot fix it up and sell it or rent it out, it is not an investment, it's a gamble. And that's the case if you got it for ten cents on the dollar or fifty cents on the dollar.

KEY INSIGHT

An exit strategy provides a course of action that's designed to make you money. When you buy a "deal" you invest in that exit strategy. Anything less is speculation. It can pay off, but speculators generally lose more money than they make. Why take that chance in a market where knowledgeable investors are telling you there is money to be made without extra risk?

IDENTIFY YOUR EXIT STRATEGY

There are three real estate investment markets where you can make money: the fix-and-flip, the long-term rental, and the wholesale market. In the latter, you buy deeply discounted homes to sell to other investors. When you're choosing an exit strategy that focuses on one of these market niches, remember that while each can make you money, their potential differs depending on what stage of the real estate cycle that market is in. (See Insight 16: Understand the Real Estate Cycle.) In light of the current market situation, let's zero in on the part of the real estate cycle where the investment opportunities are driven by two factors: discount prices and high foreclosure rates.

We know those two factors contribute to your ability to find a good deal. At this stage in the market, all three exit strategies can work, assuming you have a buyer or renter who wants that property. But there's no question one exit strategy is especially well-suited to these market conditions, and that's the buy-and-hold exit strategy.

Before we look at why the buy-and-hold strategy is particularly advantageous in this market, let's dig beneath some of the common mis-conceptions about using the wholesale and buy-and-flip market at this stage in the real estate cycle. A lot of inexperienced investors (or those who don't pay close enough attention to market fundamentals) say their exit strategy is based on the wholesale market. They plan to flip the property to another investor (one who'll do the required property upgrades) and while they'll only make a few thousand dollars on the deal, this strategy quickly frees up their time and money. Others say that their exit strategy involves buying a discounted property, fixing it up, and flipping it back onto the resale market.

Both are workable strategies. Both also can be more difficult to put into play than the short-sighted investor might think. For one thing, both strategies require a buyer. No problem, since you're in a buyer's market, right? Wrong! Because you are selling into a buyer's market, your position is naturally compromised. There may well be money to be made, but it's risky because buyers are inundated with choice.

KEY INSIGHT

The buy-renovate-flip-market is a serious business because every month your investment stays on the market is another month its mort-gage stays on your books. Understand that staged homes sell 50 percent quicker than non-staged homes, so seriously consider staging your home for the retail sale market. Hire a professional staging com-pany or, if you have an eye for decorating, do it yourself. The biggest thing to remember: less is more! Keep the furniture and decorations to a minimum, so potential buyers see liveable space and not clutter.

Why Buy-and-Hold Makes Sense

Once a market-smart investor realizes the risks of selling into a buyer's market, she may develop her deals a little differently. In this current market, the best exit strategy is to be found in the buy-and-hold market. That potentially means a long-term relationship with property managers who know what they're doing and tenants who respond to being treated well. This adds up to years of stable cash-flowing revenue. But most importantly, down markets go up, so investors who buy and rent properties will also benefit from their property's appreciation. Here, the exit strategy looks ahead to a time when prices are rising and fewer houses are on the market.

Our main point is that the buy-and-hold strategy is successful when applied to neighborhoods with a stable tenant market and steady demand for rental properties. This strategy also exemplifies what smart investors talk about when they say they are after the "patient money." What they advocate meets market fundamentals because they buy at a discount in a buyer's market, rent the property for good cash flow, allow the market cycle to do what it has always done, and then sell when the market shows clear signs of being a seller's market. In fact, that's where some investors discipline themselves to be even more patient. Instead of selling early in the seller's market of the real estate cycle, they hold onto their properties longer than planned because inflation has kicked their rents so high they don't want to give up the healthy cash flow.

If you've purchased a property in the right way—with cash flow— and property values go up, you have to consider the capital gains payable on the sale, in which case it may not be advantageous for you to sell. Buy and hold means that you buy a solid residential income-producing property, which could end up becoming "pool side revenue."

KEY INSIGHT

If you can make more money by revising your exit strategy, then go ahead. Just avoid having to change your strategy so that you lose less!

WHOLESALE AND FIX-AND-FLIP OPTIONS

The wisdom of patient money aside, some investors will stick to the wholesale or fix-and-flip markets and it's clear that both can make you money. But be careful. These markets are often perceived (and aggressively marketed) as "easier" because they appear to demand less commitment (you won't have to deal with property management issues). Reality paints a different picture. First, the historic number of distressed properties on the market means there are more houses than buyers. Be honest about what that means. The opportunities are there, but buyers—including investors—can afford to be picky. Unless your properties are deeply discounted and located in prime neighborhoods, you will have trouble finding buyers as there is a much greater chance they will be able to find better deals in better areas.

To make wholesale deals work, you need a business strategy that includes a good relationship with a group of investors. You also need to know reliable real estate owned (REO) agents (who typically work for lenders) and others who can find you these deals, cheap. You'll need tips on when auctions are going to be held, when REO houses will be on the market and, ideally, a way to find out when homeowners want to discount a property for a quick sale to ward off the foreclosure process.

Even with all that background work, the investment facts remain the same. If you pay too much for a distressed property and set the wholesale price too high, you might get stuck with the property. As it's currently more difficult for Canadians to finance the wholesale deal, carrying a property for longer than anticipated can cause big problems for your next deal, too.

Canadians who want to get into the wholesale and fixer-upper retail markets also should be aware that the most successful wholesalers and property flippers live in the markets where they work. This gives them critical and timely access to buyers and sellers.

KEY INSIGHT

If you don't plan to live in the market where you're buying real estate investment property, think twice about the wholesale and fix-and-flip niches. Once you get a reliable team on the ground, these markets can be quite manageable, but other investors and those selling distressed properties will not wait for you to fly in when local investors have properties to buy and sell.

Recognize that financing is more difficult on the wholesale and residential retail markets. If you decide to fix and flip homes into the first-time homebuyer market, you will need to understand how federal assistance mortgages work.

Historically speaking, Federal Housing Administration (FHA) loans have allowed lower-income Americans to borrow money to buy a home when they cannot afford a conventional down payment or do not qualify for private mortgage insurance (PMI). Veterans Affairs (VA) home loans play a similar role for veterans, active duty personnel, reservists and National Guard members, and some surviving spouses. Canadians in this market must understand that FHA and VA financing are the most active loans in the nation right now.

Besides understanding that your market targets people who qualify for FHA and VA loans, you will need to fine-tune your marketing plan to meet the needs of the first-time homebuyer. While you may think it's enough to market on price, these buyers are not familiar with the market, and they respond much more quickly to information about "how much down and how much a month."

US market insiders say that property condition in the current fix-and-flip market is also very important; to make a sale, the property must be stellar and stand out from competing inventory. As the success of this exit strategy hinges on the quick sale, you also may need a more aggressive marketing program that uses everything from lawn signs to what the industry calls "bandit signs," which are eye-catching signs posted in high-traffic areas.

Working with a top-notch real estate agent is another way to push your house to the market. In addition to costing you a commission (arguably a good use of someone else's time!), you will need to be in close contact with that agent to make sure your house is being marketed aggressively.

PICK YOUR PARTNERS CAREFULLY

There's no question that a hot market attracts money. Before you hand over any investment cash, make sure you know what you're getting! Some investors already doing business in the US market have proven track records and do high-volume business. That's a good starting point. Also look for good contacts with local investor groups and buyers—you want to make sure your partners have a team on the ground before you invest with a particular company.

Again, this is a buyer's market. It's relatively easy to acquire and upgrade property, and if you've got an influx of cash, you can do a lot of deals. But do you want to get into a large-volume market that makes your money swim against the real estate cycle's current? Absolutely not. You want to partner on deals that sell and that require people on the ground that are familiar with that market. What works in one part of Arizona may not work in another part of the same state, let alone California, Florida, or Nevada.

CHOOSE AN EXIT STRATEGY THAT MAKES MONEY

A smart investor once said that no man is bigger than the market. E.W. Howe summed it up a little differently when he wrote, "No man's credit is as good as his money." These sayings address two of the central points about investing in the US distressed property market. First, you can make money there, and second, you can lose money there. As an investor, you want to stay on the positive side of the investment ledger.

To do that, swim with the current. In the real estate investment market right now, that means focusing on the buy-and-hold side of the market. It's a niche where you can develop a volume business with less risk, all because the market fundamentals are so positive. As long as you're paying attention to where you're buying, there is no shortage of renters. As long as you're attentive to how much you're paying, there are good opportunities for cash flow. With good management and some patience, your "patient money" properties can develop future wealth.

15

Know Your Financing Options and Obstacles

Financing is another investment fundamental Canadians need to understand as they research the US foreclosures market. While a lot of Canadians are bringing their own capital to this market, others are wisely looking at financing as a way to put someone else's money to work on their deals. Where can you find money and how does it work?

The news is not all good. If you're looking for financing, you'll soon find that the US options for Canadians and other foreign real estate investors wanting to buy US property are scarce. For Canadians, there are banks in the United States that are willing to lend to Canadians with 20 to 35 percent down when they purchase a second home for personal use. But what you won't find are many lenders willing to advance funds for the purchase of investment properties.

This is surprising for a lot of investors—the same lenders that deny dollars to international borrowers also say that foreign investment can revive American real estate markets. To understand what's going on, Canadians should know a bit about what's behind the massive downturn in the American real estate market.

It all goes back to the Federal National Mortgage Association (FNMA), known as Fannie Mae, and the Federal Home Loan Mortgage Corporation (FHLMC), known as Freddie Mac. These stockholder-owned corporations were set up by US Congress in the late 1960s to purchase and provide some security for mortgages and ensure funds were consistently available to the institutions that lent money to homebuyers.

In essence, these were two government-backed mortgage agencies and they held almost all of the mortgage loans in the United States. The banks that you may be trying to meet with now (Wells Fargo, Bank of America, and JP Morgan Chase, for example) sell their mortgages to FNMA and FHLMC. Fannie Mae and Freddie Mac made the rules on what types of loans were acceptable and they didn't buy mortgages from lenders who didn't stick within their guidelines. That hasn't changed, and since Fannie and Freddie currently hold that international investor loans are too risky, lenders won't lend foreigners investment money.

Fannie Mae and Freddie Mac argue that international investor loans are too risky if the borrower doesn't have a US FICO score (credit rating). They also take issue with the complications of verifying foreign income and assets and argue that if an international borrower defaults, it's too hard to chase them for recourse on the loan.

That rationale ignores the validity of reliable credit ratings available in countries like Canada. It also dismisses the potential to decrease the risk of default by requiring international investors to put down more money. (An investor with 50 percent down has some real skin in the deal and is less likely to default. That's how basic investment math works.) Fannie and Freddie's approach also discounts the fact that today's US housing prices reflect such a significant market downturn that many properties are substantially undervalued. The ability to buy an investment property at such deep discounts protects the investment risk. Lenders could also implement a faster foreclosure process against non-US residents.

The legitimacy of these arguments aside, that's not what is happening in the US market, where Americans with a "fair" credit rating can borrow money for their primary residence and put down 3.5 percent.

This is a message Canadian investors need to speak up about when they're looking to invest in the US market. The more Americans who hear this message, the greater the likelihood that the people at Fannie Mae and Freddie Mac will wake up and realize that they can't trumpet that foreign investors can save the US real estate market without supporting foreign investors with fair and competitive financing.

Looking ahead, we suspect financing options will improve in the future, because that's what happens when a real estate market cycles back after a correction. If US money is critical to your deal, however, you've got work to do. But American market insiders say changes to the foreign investor lending rules aren't likely in the foreseeable future.

PORTFOLIO LOANS

In the meantime, though, how do you get some US financing for your deals if your options with mortgages bought by the Fannie Mae and Freddie Mac group do not look promising? *Portfolio loans* (mortgages held for the long term, usually by smaller local banks) represent a small percentage of housing loans not sold to Fannie and Freddie. Since they are not trying to sell mortgage paper to Fannie and Freddie, they do not have to follow their guidelines.

This is a good place to start your search for a US investment loan. Begin with smaller local banks that do portfolio loans in the area where you are looking to invest.

To be straight, a lot of them will turn you down and probably for the same reasons the FNMA guidelines suggest. But be diligent. Find smaller local banks that work outside the FNMA box and start building relationships with people who may be able to look at your deals on a case-by-case basis. If you're serious about accessing US financing, be very professional. Make sure you know what you're asking for and be prepared to show these banks how you'll deliver their money, with interest.

PRIVATE MONEY

Private money, also known as *hard money*, is another option. Just like private money works "outside the box," these lenders do loans to foreign investors. When compared to bank financing, these funds can be easier to get and harder to pay off, so be careful.

Finding sources of private money is relatively easy. Private lenders can be found in most of the big markets through advertisements, real estate investment association clubs, real estate agents, and title companies who work with investors. As always, relationships are important, so ask around and find out who knows whom.

Keep in mind that a private lender will tend to lend based on the deal itself versus the borrower. This is why private money is almost always higher in fees and the interest rates can be double or triple what a bank charges. In the current market, foreign investors can expect to be charged borrower fees plus interest rates starting at about 6 percent.

With a sound exit strategy (see Insight 14), private money can be an ideal way to finance a fixer-upper in the short term. (Remember, even if you can get bank financing, most banks will not loan money on a house that needs major rehab work. With the right deal, this is where private money can help.) However, carrying the property with such a high interest rate for too long can hurt cash flow or resale profits. As well, most of these loans stipulate a one-year term, so a good exit strategy is vital.

One good thing about using private money is that it can provide good leverage to get you into a property and give you time to season a property. *Seasoning* is the term banks use to describe a property that's been owned for a certain period of time. A seasoned property can make a bank feel more comfortable about loaning on the property. For a property to be considered seasoned a bank usually wants to see that someone has owned it for one year or more. (A few banks will consider six months to be a sufficient seasoning period.)

This is important because you may be able to use private money to secure a property after it has been seasoned for a year and then refinance the home with a local bank that does portfolio loans. But that refinancing "possibility" is not a detail you can leave to chance, especially when you most likely will need to repay that private loan after twelve months. Remember, hard-money lenders are not afraid to take your property. If the term of the loan is only one year and you can't pay it off when that year is up, the private money lender can choose to extend the loan for you or take the property back. So if you plan to use private money with this strategy in mind, start interviewing local banks before you use the private money and make sure you have a backup plan in place to pay off the private loan. That also may be possible through an equity line of credit on a Canadian property or by using cash reserves you have on the sidelines.

KEY INSIGHT

If you're looking for US financing for your American deals, proceed with caution. Your plan to get the money has to include a plan to pay it back, especially if you're using private financing.

You do not want to pay premium interest rates on a private loan for twelve months—and then lose the property as well.

LEVERAGE YOUR CANADIAN SUCCESSES

Another viable option involves leveraging off a *lowly geared* (low debt-to-value) property you own in Canada. Here, you use that property to take out an equity line or a second mortgage and apply that money to financing a property you buy in the United States. As long as the property you buy has a healthy cash flow, it should cover the debt service for the money you borrow. (You could also leverage a US mortgage, although that's going to be more difficult to access in the first place given the Fannie Mae/Freddie Mac rules.)

KEY INSIGHT

Robust real estate investment markets are no excuse for putting your Canadian assets at risk, and market veterans with integrity would never encourage you to over-leverage any property, because hard cash is always better than new debt. Again, do not confuse money-making strategies with "sure things." In real estate, as in life, there are no sure things!

16

Understand the Real Estate Cycle

The current buzz of media stories and investment gossip about the US distressed property market was predated by a whole lot of attention to real estate market booms, busts, and bubbles. If you pay any attention to the real estate investment market, you know the "three Bs" garner a whole lot of attention when people are trying to figure out what's going on in the market. What they're really looking for is information about *why* a market is acting the way it is at a particular moment in time. Why are prices so high or so low? Why are so many homes on the market? Why are there more buyers than sellers or vice versa?

Smart investors think differently. Instead of asking why a market is acting a particular way, ask where a market is at in the "real estate cycle." This information answers all of the questions above in terms of how a market is behaving. Better yet, it will guide your investment acquisitions and fine-tune your exit strategies.

KEY INSIGHT

Think of the real estate cycle as a circle of activity that spins in one direction. Fortunes are made and lost as the cycle revolves, but there is money to be made at every point. This is possible because smart investors invest with the cycle's momentum. They go with the current to reap bigger rewards and minimize their risks.

For example, the real estate cycle offers insight into what happened in the US market to contribute to the current situation where we have record numbers of distressed properties on the market. The cycle doesn't predict when a cycle might change, but those familiar with how it works will see indications of an impending shift from recovery to boom or boom to slump. History shows that a lot of people familiar with the real estate cycle were asking questions about the US real estate market by 2006. They wondered how long the boom was going to last and, by default, what events might precipitate a market crash and how bad things might be when the boom ended.

WHAT IS THE REAL ESTATE CYCLE?

The real estate cycle (which occurs on both sides of the Canada–US border) was first identified more than seventy years ago by Homer Hoyt, the man now called the grandfather of the real estate cycle concept. In 1933, Hoyt analyzed a century of movement in Chicago's land values and documented his findings in his book, *One Hundred Years of Land Values in Chicago*, published by University of Chicago Press. In the book, Hoyt documented how a recurrent succession of causes and effects impacted land values from 1830 to 1930. In sum, he recognized a big-picture pattern at play and detailed how that pattern affected the real estate market.

Subsequent studies support Hoyt's contention of a recurrent succession of causes and effects impacting land values. We now understand that the real estate cycle follows a consistent pattern that moves through three basic stages of what's called the *real estate cycle clock*. These stages are recovery, boom, and slump.

The clock's timing can be somewhat irregular and even volatile, but the fundamental pattern remains the same; that is, the recovery, boom, and slump pattern always repeats itself, but the time frame of each phase in the cycle is not consistent with previous cycles. The timing is based on the simple laws of supply and demand. By knowing what factors affect those forces you can find genuine predictive value in the real estate cycle, making understanding it one of your real estate investment fundamentals.

Before we look at how to recognize these three phases, let's talk about some of the factors that contribute to the movement from one phase to another. They are known as the key drivers and market influencers.

Key Drivers and Market Influencers

Key drivers propel the real estate market through the various phases of the real estate cycle. Some of these key drivers are volatile and others are more stable. Regardless, it is the collective impact of key drivers that a real estate investor has to watch. While no single key driver can move the real estate cycle through a complete phase on its own, the right combination of drivers can have a major impact. The key drivers can be divided into three categories: demographic, financial, and emotional.

Demographic

- Net migration/population growth
- Real estate vacancy rates
- Employment
- Real estate construction
- Number of people per household

Financial

- Real estate return on investment (ROI)
- Rents
- Incomes
- Real estate financing availability
- Gross domestic product
- Real estate values
- Real estate affordability

Emotional

- Number of days to sell real estate
- Gentrification
- Real estate listings
- Real estate sales

Demographic changes, such as population growth, can quickly increase demand for real estate. Other key drivers are financial changes, such as an increase in the level of rents, which affect the viability of real estate investments. And other key drivers, like the number of days it takes to sell real estate, can induce panic buying when buyers are driven by the fear of missing out during the boom phase of the real estate cycle. If population growth, an increase in rent levels, and panic buying occur simultaneously, their impact on the real estate cycle is more immediate.

Market influencers are factors that affect the perception of the length of a specific phase of the real estate cycle. It is important to understand that these market influencers are often confused with key drivers. But unlike drivers, which actually move the real estate cycle from one phase to another, market influencers affect the immediate levels of supply and demand in the real estate market. Their impact, however, is temporary.

Real estate investors need to recognize how the temporary nature of market influencers impact the cycle by giving a false impression of where a cycle is moving. Market influencers do not drive the real estate cycle from one phase to the next, but create the illusion of that happening. The great news about market influencers is that they can set up a window of opportunity for prudent investors. These opportunities arise as a direct result of the confusion created by the market influencers in terms of what is really happening in the market.

KEY INSIGHT

Students of the real estate cycle can capitalize on the short-term effects of market influencers because they recognize how temporary blips in the market create short-term opportunities to acquire property or execute an exit strategy.

Classic market influencers that can temporarily shift a real estate cycle include the following:

- Interest rates (the cost of finance)

- Ease of borrowing (the availability of finance)

- Confidence in real estate as an investment vehicle

- Inflation

- Legislative amendments (taxation and/or local authority)

- Investment alternatives

BOOM, SLUMP, AND RECOVERY

The three phases of the market cycle—boom, slump, and recovery—can be identified by specific things that happen in the market during these periods. Investors can use that information to figure out where a particular market is at on the real estate cycle.

Boom

The boom phase tends to be the shortest phase in the real estate cycle (although anomalies do happen). At this phase, capital growth is the name of the game. There are more buyers than sellers in the market and this forces up prices. Property values also increase—slowly at the start of the boom, and gather impressive speed as this stage progresses. The boom phase nears completion when prices reach their maximum.

During a boom, the public is very positive about buying property. Booms are characterized by a high volume of sales and quick-selling properties. As properties are snapped up soon after they go onto the market, the boom phase sets the stage for relatively fewer listings.

At this point, the sellers have the negotiating power. More and more people focus on adding value to their properties and this continues until the end of the boom. Rents also increase during the early stages of a boom. As the rents rise, the number of people living in each dwelling also increases as it becomes harder for people to afford to rent.

About midway through this phase, rents peak. That affects the return investors are able to get on their buy-and-hold property investments, and with property values still rising, rents cannot keep pace.

Slump

In the slump phase, the increase in property values slows and may come to a halt as the supply of property exceeds demand. Sometimes values even recede, although this doesn't happen in every slump or in every area. By the end of the slump phase, values are at their most affordable levels for that phase of the cycle.

With property supply exceeding demand, buyers now have the negotiating edge. It takes longer and longer to sell property and agents have more listings than in other phases of the real estate cycle. As fewer properties sell during a slump than at any other time, investors will notice that the same real estate agents who happily ignored them during the boom now start to return phone calls. Some of the best property-buying opportunities arise during this period as vendors are motivated and purchasers have an extraordinary amount of control.

Recovery

As a market enters the recovery phase, the rental population starts to increase, resulting in a shortage of rental property. Property values also begin to rise slowly and investors get a better return on investment as rents rise and vacancy rates start to fall. Interest rates are attractive and financing becomes easier to get as banks come under pressure to lend so they can capitalize on the increased need for borrowing.

First-time homebuyers become more active in this market, but fear still rules with memories of price corrections in the preceding slump. As the recovery phase progresses, experienced investors recognize the potential for increased returns and enter the market aggressively. Inexperienced investors remain cautious, most wanting to wait to see what happens before they take any action.

The recovery phase is also characterized by increased construction of new dwellings, as builders and developers start new projects, and many property owners add value to their properties. Throughout the recovery phase, property values rise, but media reports reflect low confidence in real estate as an investment. The end of the recovery phase often blurs with the beginning of the next boom, and it can be hard to tell when the cycle is changing.

RECOGNIZING CYCLE SHIFTS

Investors tuned in to the real estate cycle watch for signs of a shift from one phase to the next and use that information to guide purchase decisions and exit strategies. They balance cash flow and appreciation with long-term wealth building.

From Slump to Recovery: Opportunity Thrives

At the beginning of the slump phase, property values may still be rising, though at slower rates. Property sales volumes fall from their former heights and there is a lower ROI. This is accompanied by increased holding costs. Many investors consider selling a property or two, which signals a further market shift as the increased number of sellers compete with each other. This further floods the market with properties for sale.

Midway through the slump there is an abundance of motivated vendors who were forced to sell their properties because of low returns and high holding costs. The media bashes real estate and fear rules the day as people worry about short-term equity corrections. Employment levels are low at this stage and financing is harder to get.

As the slump nears its end, unemployment is at its peak, population growth and income levels are at their lowest, and rents remain fairly static. At the end of the slump, values are low and vendors are increasingly desperate.

This is the stage of the real estate cycle that wise investors have been waiting for! With very few buyers in the market now, there is less competition for you as an investor. Take note of words like "urgent" in property advertisements. In this phase, it takes longer and longer to sell properties, but you will start to see more first-time homebuyers entering the market. Even though the media is still reporting doom and gloom as far as property is concerned, these buyers are focusing on what they can afford.

KEY INSIGHT

What motivates first-time homebuyers as a market moves from slump to recovery? With rents holding steady, this market segment starts to do the basic math. They don't ask if they can afford the asking price, they ask if they can afford the monthly payments.

Key Recovery Signs Checklist

❏ Population increasing

❏ New construction starting

❏ Financing more accessible

❏ Rents rising

❏ Property values increasing

❏ Returns increasing

❏ Property sellers dropping prices to compete with the rising number of properties on the market

From Recovery to Boom: Concerns Give Way to Prosperity

As the recovery gives way to a boom, investors notice an increase in the rental population accompanied by rising employment and income levels. Rents are going up and property values are rising. This means investors are getting a greater ROI on properties they already own. The returns on new properties are often lower at the start of a boom because increases in rent are unable to keep up with increases in property values.

During the initial stages of a boom, much of the public holds "anti-real estate" feelings because of the previous slump, and most fail to recognize quickly that the boom is already underway. At the same time, more people start entering the real estate market, driving up property prices.

By the middle of the boom, the increase in rents reaches a peak and vacancy levels are still low. Values continue to rise and property sells quickly. It is easy to get financing; banks are relaxed about allowing people to borrow to the absolute maximum they can afford. At mid-boom, everyone from the neighbors to the taxi driver is talking about the benefits of real estate investments, as is the media. New investors enter the market, egged on by the general excitement level and an increased awareness of real estate investment seminars (see Insight 11).

Unfortunately, greed is the flavor of the day. You will notice a great deal of speculation; buyers are buying property based on plans versus built product. As the end of the boom nears, population growth slows and the ratio of buyers to sellers in the market starts to level out. People also are finding it harder to meet their mortgage payments and this slows down the boom's momentum.

Key Boom Signs Checklist

❏ Increasing population

❏ Increasing employment

❏ Increasing incomes

❏ Increasing rents

❏ Increasing property values

❏ High, easy property sales

❏ More accessible financing

❏ Increasing construction

❏ Greed

From Boom to Slump: Buyers Struggle with Affordability

Looking back to 2006, real estate investors who were tuned in to the real estate cycle saw how key drivers and market influencers were pushing a market boom towards a slump. The key driver in this latest US market slump was definitely the credit crisis. That occurred as demand plunged in many over-built markets where housing prices had moved well beyond market affordability. Real estate investors who pulled their money out before the slump are now putting that money back in, in anticipation of the market recovery.

Brilliant. But it's not rocket science; it's the real estate cycle!

Key Slump Signs Checklist

❏ Low to no population growth

❏ Increasing unemployment

❏ Decreasing incomes

❏ Oversupply of property

❏ Less accessible financing

❏ Decreasing or flat rents

❏ Decreasing or flat property values

❏ Desperate vendors.

17

Find the People Who Can Help You Find Foreclosures

Have you heard the story of the out-of-shape person who approaches a highly regarded personal trainer for some help getting back into shape? The individual tells the trainer that all he needs to know is "the best way to get into great shape."

The trainer tells him, "No problem! I know exactly how you can do it!" The client is thrilled. "Great!" says the out-of-shape person. "What's the secret?"

"Consistent diet and exercise," answers the personal trainer.

"Yeah, okay . . . But besides that?" is the disappointed response from the client.

We share this story because it reflects a common problem that is raised when talking to new real estate investors and people who want to be real estate investors. Instead of focusing on what's effective and proven to work, they avoid the obvious because it all seems like too much work.

Well, here's the deal. Real estate investing takes work even if you've decided to focus on the US foreclosure market, which is rife with opportunity. We know that everyone wants a fancy and sexy shortcut, but those shortcuts usually just run you in circles. So lose the attitude that screams, "If something is not clever, it can't work!" Real estate investing works. But there's no magic.

THE NOT-SO-SECRET WAY TO FIND GREAT REAL ESTATE DEALS

The first thing you need to find good real estate investment deals for distressed properties in the US market are good relationships with top-notch real estate agents, *wholesalers* (individuals who focus on the quick-turn or "flip" real estate deal), and the people you meet through real estate investment associations.

This people-centered approach celebrates the fact that real estate investment is a relationship business. And the strategy here is simple: you can spend your time and money on fancy mailings and other programs that are designed to help you find property deals, or you can use real estate professionals and real estate investment organizations to the same end. Maybe you want to stick with the strategy that puts other people to work for you.

KEY INSIGHT

Canadian real estate investors can find lots of people who are willing to sell them foolproof marketing programs that will bring US foreclosure deals to the front doors of your Canadian offices. Save your money. Use a real estate agent to find deals. It's less expensive, less time-consuming, and usually way more effective. It's also likely to work in all markets.

UNDERSTAND WHAT AN AGENT CAN DO FOR YOUR BUSINESS

If you plan to buy investment property in more than one market, you're going to need real estate agents and wholesalers in each of those markets. What works in California may not get any response in Florida or Nevada, since effective marketing and advertising programs can vary greatly from area to area.

Your goal is to have an experienced real estate agent and wholesaler provide you with good deals at a discount within the niche type of house you aim to buy. To make that happen, you should definitely look for real estate owned (REO) real estate agents. They've been hired by the bank to resell properties the bank has foreclosed on. As banks are the most motivated sellers on the market right now (see Insight 7), an REO agent will also be motivated to make a deal.

KEY INSIGHT

Not every discounted property is a good deal. Make that your mantra! Never make a deal unless you know how the market fundamentals affect the investment potential of a particular property. You don't want to buy in the wrong area, or buy a home that needs significant upgrades unless the discounted price *and* market fundamentals tell you the deal makes sense.

One US investor says that in one city in Florida, there are a handful of agents who handle the majority of all the REO listings. These agents do volume and are no-nonsense. Because their time is in high demand, you can't expect them to go out to long lunches with an investor the first time you meet.

GETTING AN REO AGENT'S ATTENTION

As a newcomer to the US distressed property market, Canadian investors have to realize that REOs in some areas are inundated with investor queries. Since they probably are already working with a network of investors, you'll need to get their attention if you want in on the deals they're involved with.

How do you do that? There are three magic statements that will help you get your foot in the door with REOs.

I Will Not Waste Your Time

Say this when you first meet the REO—and mean it. Tell them exactly what kind of deal you are looking for. Skip the list of questions from the last investing book you read and be natural and friendly. You want to let them know that you know what you're doing and what you're looking for.

People do business with people they know, like, and trust. Build that rapport. Let the REO agent know that you need to buy at a discount to make the numbers work for you and be specific about the type of property you are looking for. (See the list at the end of this Insight.)

I Have the Funds Ready to Close the Deal

REO agents really dislike it when someone puts a house under contract and the deal doesn't close. Let them know that you have access to cash. It might even be smart to give them proof of funds the first time you meet. This could be a credit statement, a bank account statement, or an approval letter from a local hard-money lender. If you don't have any of this yet, don't worry. Just assure the REO with confidence that you can perform, and then follow through.

I Always Give You Both Sides of the Commission

This point is huge. Money talks. Period. Let the agent know right up front that you are not working with a buyer's agent and you want them to keep all of the commission. REO agents work hard to get their listing from banks and obviously would prefer to keep more commission.

If you are an agent, be prepared to forego your commission. You will make your money on the deal, so don't compromise your working relationship with an REO.

KEY INSIGHT

Canadian investors who are serious about the US foreclosure market must recognize the value of being able to make and follow through on these three statements. With perseverance and honesty, you can use this strategy to open a virtual pipeline of future profits. Once you're serious about a market, politely stay in contact with your REOs. If a deal comes up that really fits your parameters, buy it. That kind of follow-through shows you are serious.

Canadian investors sometimes worry it will be difficult to find the larger-volume REO agents in an area, but they're unlikely to have that problem. As part of your market due diligence, you need to talk to real estate agents and property managers. Ask them who's doing the REO business and look on sites like Realtor.com.

You can also call different real estate offices in the area and ask to speak with the broker/manager. Tell them you want to work with an agent who meets these criteria:

- Specializes with investors, distressed property sales, and foreclosures

- Has been in the market for at least five years

- Owns his or her own investment property

This won't always yield a good referral. But it does get you talking to people who are active in the local real estate market. As you interview them and talk about the market, you'll get a better feel for the area. You'll also start to get the kind of information you need to compare agents.

It goes without saying that you should never feel obligated to buy a house from an agent whom you've just interviewed. But do be fair with the agent's time. There is nothing wrong with asking an agent to send you some potential listings to look over. Just don't forget that this is a relationship business. You want to cultivate relationships with people that you really want to work with.

BEYOND THE REO

Agents other than REO agents can also find deals for you. *Short sales*, where the owner and lender are highly motivated to sell before a formal foreclosure action, abound in this market, and a knowledgeable agent can help you identify good deals and put in offers. Short sales can be tricky, so make sure your agent and the listing agent are absolute bulldogs with staying on top of the bank. As we talked about in Insight 9, the odds of getting a short-sale property are very low. So if a property really fits your system, make sure the deal goes through.

KEY INSIGHT

Investors make their money on deals, not almost-deals. If an agent brings you listings that are far outside the parameters of the deals you've asked them to be on the lookout for, find out what's happening. Either they weren't listening, don't get it or don't care.

Relationships are a two-way street. If one side isn't working, look somewhere else.

CHECK OUT THE WHOLESALER MARKET

Wholesalers are remarkably different from real estate agents. The good ones are savvy investors who have close relationships with REO agents and banks. Because they buy volume, and volume has its privileges, a lot of wholesalers are first in line for great deals.

And why shouldn't they be? They buy at the auction steps, they buy REO, they buy short sales. Ideally, they aim to buy deals low, and turn around and sell them right away to other investors at wholesale prices. Most will try to tack on price increases of at least $10,000 higher than what they paid.

One US insider says he works with wholesalers who will sell him property at $4,000 above what they paid. That discount is based on the fact that this investor buys a steady volume of property from the same wholesalers—and he always closes his deals. The bottom line is that he gets the house at a price that works for him with very little effort. Again, you can chalk that up to relationships.

Double-Check the Wholesaler's Numbers

If you want to deal in the wholesale market, understand that wholesalers will buy property anywhere in town and they then will sell that property for as much as they can get. It's up to you to decide whether a particular deal works for you. Always do the math and know your market fundamentals, because some of their deals are good and some are not.

As with any vendor, real estate investors must never take a wholesaler's word on property values, the costs of repairs, or the going rental rates. In fact, if you're doing business in the United States you must be wary of the numbers you get from a wholesaler, especially if this market is new to you. In a business where cash is king, a wholesaler does not have to do your homework!

Investors also must be on guard for what the industry terms *fake wholesalers*. These are the guys who get listings from real wholesalers, tack on a few more thousand dollars to the deal, and try to sell it to you at the higher price. This isn't illegal. But the more middlemen involved with a deal, the higher the end price. If you're serious about the wholesale market, aim to buy from the original wholesaler.

A Word About Accents

The Canadian accent is recognizable in the United States, and as soon as the people you're dealing with realize you're not a local, they may test your market knowledge and try to make you pay extra. To find a reputable wholesaler, ask around. Title companies, real estate agents, property managers, and hard-money lenders are high on the list of people you need to meet, so get them to help you learn your way around a local market.

KEY INSIGHT

Trust but verify. Every property you look at is being marketed as a great deal. Run your own numbers because it's up to you to decide if they're realistic.

DEAL FLOW

Once you've established a working relationship with REO agents and wholesalers, don't just sit back. You need to stay in touch with these people and you can't expect them to be calling you. Proactive follow-up is key!

You also can expect to spend a fair bit of time reviewing deals, crunching the numbers on potential properties, inspecting homes, and checking various market fundamentals. Like the diet and exercise prescribed in the opening anecdote, this kind of due diligence is what will keep your business on track for success.

In addition, new investors must steel themselves against the flood of emotions that comes on as deals come and go. With experience, you'll learn that potential deals are like windows of opportunity. Some open, some close, and some slip through the cracks, but that's okay. Persistence pays off.

A RECIPE FOR SUCCESS

Canadians interested in the US real estate market often ask what experienced US investors are looking for when they buy property. Here's what an American market specialists says to watch for:

- Three or four bedrooms with two baths
- Block, brick, or new construction
- Priced below the median value for the area
- 1,200 to 2,000 square feet
- 1-percent marker with fair taxes and insurance
- Starter-home neighborhood
  - mixture of renters and owners
  - easy-to-manage areas

- Proximity to job sources

- Tenants with replaceable income

- Rents matching government rent rates (monthly mortgage payment within $200 of the rent rate if the home had been purchased at full market value by a first-time homebuyer)

- The ability to buy at a discount.

18

Benefit from the Five Profit Centers of Real Estate

In real estate markets like this, it's easy for Canadians who want to invest in US distressed property to think they can skip over a few of the investment fundamentals. To adjust this misguided thinking, let's talk about profit centers.

A *profit center* is a source through which you generate a gain. Real estate has five profit centers:

- Natural appreciation

- Forced appreciation

- Positive cash flow

- Mortgage reduction and leverage

- Tax deductions

Investors who understand the profit centers of real estate optimize their ability to put different profit centers to work in their portfolios. The more you understand about how these profit centers work, the less likely you'll miss out on an opportunity to profit—or focus on one profit center when another one is better. A sound understanding of profit centers also will help you adopt and fine-tune exit strategies.

KEY INSIGHT

Most investments only have one or two profit centers. Stocks typically have a dividend component (periodic cash distribution) and a capital gain component. That's two profit centers. Real estate has five.

NATURAL APPRECIATION

Natural appreciation is often called market appreciation. It's the gradual inflation in real estate values over time. Some "hot" markets appreciate faster than others and some do not appreciate at all (but that's rare and usually speaks to other issues, like property degradation or a serious problem with location).

The rate of natural appreciation in Canadian residential real estate over the last fifty years has been just over 6 percent per year. This is a national average and many markets are above or below this. Still, it illustrates that real estate values generally rise over time.

The main factor driving this is inflation in the value of the land. While buildings depreciate over time, the value of the land increases. Research shows that land typically increases in value faster than the consumer price index (CPI) or general inflation in consumer goods. This makes land (and the property that sits on it) an excellent investment and hedge against inflation.

We also know that the purchasing power of money degrades over time, so having your money invested into an appreciating asset is a smart way to maintain and grow the purchasing power of your money.

KEY INSIGHT

Natural appreciation is an investor's dream when you're buying in a down market.

FORCED APPRECIATION

Forced appreciation is one of the most powerful aspects of real estate. This is an increase in value that you create through upgrades and renovations. Forced appreciation is entirely within the property owner's control. Whereas natural appreciation speaks to market forces, forced appreciation is a way to increase the value of your property even during a down market or flat cycle.

But the potential for forced appreciation depends on buying the right property. This is a fundamental truism. If you've bought a brand-new penthouse condominium there may be nothing you can do to improve the property in the short term. The same holds for other "traditional" investments since you can't add a basement suite to your mutual fund and create extra value.

Interest in this profit center is why we hear about so many fix-and-flip investors. It's also why there are so many reality TV shows about renovations. While forced appreciation is an important profit center and can allow you to make a quick buck, a strategy that targets forced appreciation also keeps you from taking advantage of the other profit centers. This is short-term gain that sacrifices long-term wealth.

KEY INSIGHT

Can't decide what to renovate, what to remove, and what to repair? Is curb appeal worth more than a bathroom do-over? Will anyone notice an aging HVAC system? Do you have to rehab the roof just because the other rental properties on the street all have new roofs? Slow down! There are smart ways to pursue forced appreciation. The Insights in Part 3 can keep your project on track and make sure your reno choices are designed to make you money.

POSITIVE CASH FLOW

As advocates of the buy-and-hold property investment, positive cash flow is our favorite profit center. *Positive cash flow* is when your rental income exceeds all of your expenses and you have a cash surplus at the end of each month. If you want to be successful in the current US market for distressed properties, this is the situation you want to shoot for. Positive cash flow is the foundation of a recurring cash influx that will allow you to achieve financial freedom.

Investors who target cash-flow properties will accelerate their wealth. First you focus on buying enough properties to cover your monthly living expenses. Several US investing colleagues say that's their definition of financial freedom. But you don't stop there. Investors who keep investing in cash-flow properties will eventually have excess cash coming in—more than they can use for their living expenses. Many will take this extra cash and reinvest it into more real estate.

The potential is limitless, but never forget how the fundamentals make a deal work. Expect cash flow to be tight when you buy. If the deal is right, cash flow will increase over time as rents rise with inflation and incomes, but your mortgage stays relatively flat. As the gap between your rent and your mortgage widens, cash flow should increase.

KEY INSIGHT

Cash flow rocks! The US market for distressed properties teems with opportunities to buy positive cash-flowing properties. Follow solid investment fundamentals. Buy the deal that works. Adopt an exit strategy that lets you take advantage of cash-flow profits. Hire capable management and keep an eye on the real estate cycle.

MORTGAGE REDUCTION AND LEVERAGE

When you buy a property and use the bank's money to finance it, this debt is eventually paid off. But it's not you who pays off the mortgage, it's the tenant! This makes a quality tenant the best business partner ever. They look after the place and pay your mortgage for you, but walk away with no financial interest in the property. If your mortgage is amortized over twenty-five years, then twenty-five years later you own the property with clear title. Although it is unlikely, the market could stay completely flat over this period and you could earn no cash flow. With mortgage reduction and leverage, however, you still wind up with a piece of real estate that you own at the end of it all.

Real estate, more so than a lot of other investments, also allows for advantaged leverage. If you walk into a bank and ask them to lend you $400,000 to invest in a business or buy shares in a corporation, they'd laugh at you and send you packing. You might be able to find a hard-money lender to lend it to you at a much higher interest rate. But if you walk into a bank and ask to borrow $400,000 to buy a $500,000 property, they're likely to play ball and lend the money to you at a good rate. With advantaged leverage, you put in $1 of your own money and earn a return on $5 because the bank puts in the extra $4.

TAX DEDUCTIONS

A lot of people find tax and accounting a really dull subject, but understanding tax laws allows you to keep more of the money you might otherwise have to pay to the government in taxes. We look at the many ways to create tax benefits in real estate more closely in Part 4, but for now, here is a little information to whet your appetite. Did you know that:

- Depreciation on the property structure can be used to shelter cash flow from tax?

- Interest on your mortgage is tax deductible? If you borrow in the United States, the interest can be deductible on your American tax return. If you borrow in Canada, the interest can be deductible on your Canadian tax return.

- Renovation work that can be properly classified as "repairs" is subject to accelerated write-off?

- Chattels like appliances and window coverings can be depreciated more quickly and used to offset tax?

And why are tax deductions a profit center? It's because successful real estate investing isn't about the money you make, it's about the money you keep. And when you're calculating cash flow and profit, the money you save on an expense is the same as making more income.

KEY INSIGHT

A lot of investors are not interested in studying and understanding tax law. The smart ones counter that by making sure they hire an accountant who specializes in real estate. If you're getting into the US market, make sure your accountant understands cross-border issues. Ignorance won't save you from double taxation, but good planning will.

19

What a Full-Service Real Estate Investment Group Offers

Full-service real estate investment groups can serve as a great stepping stone into the US foreclosure market, and Canadians who are testing the American investment waters will almost always comes across at least one of these groups. Let's be clear: full-service real estate groups have their place. But they're not all created equal and foreign investors need to do their due diligence before hooking up with a group that could spend their money without giving them anything in return!

WHAT FULL-SERVICE REAL ESTATE GROUPS DO

Full-service real estate groups are generally made up of individuals with years of experience in the market. This can be especially good in the foreclosure market, as a good full-service group will already have relationships with local real estate owned (REO) brokers, contractors, property managers, etc.

Most investors will come to a fork in the road when they choose to invest in the United States. On the one hand, there is the option for wealthy individuals with a lot of time to forge relationships with American realtors and contractors to develop what essentially is a real estate business. Or, the other option, which typically makes more sense for people, is to look for a *turnkey investment solution*. In other words, the investor purchases the property from a big or small investment group that offers all of the services needed to manage a property business. The main reason that most people will choose the second option is because they are forced to do so. American work laws prevent Canadians from doing all of the work that is required, unless Canadians obtain a work visa.

The investor should look for companies that have good financial stability, and a full team of people ready to purchase, renovate, rent, and manage the properties. These groups are currently spending a lot of time looking for foreclosures and properties to acquire, a full-time job because of the competition that is in the marketplace for purchasing these properties.

Canadians who don't want to invest on their own can leverage off a full-service team and find their way into the market with considerably less risk. The relationship also can lead to much more effective investing. Since the greatest risks in a foreclosure deal involve finding the right property, upgrading it the right way and getting it back on the market with a qualified tenant and good management in place, a good real estate group minimizes those risks. Their market knowledge translates into finding properties at deeper discounts and offering better pricing on property renovations and repairs. Ideally, a full-service group will even connect you with a quality property manager and qualified tenant—all in the same deal.

If everything goes right, the service of a full-service real estate group actually costs you nothing because the arrangement quickly takes you from zero to cash-flow investing. But let's be frank. The deal's success really hinges on whether the group sells you the house at a fair price. There are great groups out there that will get you a solid turnkey investment property at a fair price. But there are also groups that will rip you off. The good full-service real estate groups can supply you a fairly priced property that is fully renovated and located in a good area with high rental demand. It will have equity and cash flow. The property also should be occupied by a qualified tenant and under a top-notch management group that has been tested and proven.

If this is the investment route you plan to take, be careful. Here we give you some general rules for assessing the quality of a full-service group.

GOOD FULL-SERVICE REAL ESTATE GROUPS

As you work through your due diligence on a potential full-service group, you should look for a group that has a track record, has done many deals, and has an operation in place that is buying, renovating, renting, and has rental management. We tend to advise working with a larger group that has the benefits of scale, particularly with respect to the work that is required to undertake good due diligence. Generally, good full-service groups:

- Have a range of types of properties in their portfolio. You may find some specialists who work in a particular type, such as single-family homes.

- Have been active in their market for years and own investment property in that market.

- Are happy to have you visit the market and tour their business. They also are happy to supply information and answer questions.

- Do full renovations to get the property into top shape, including the roof, heating/cooling, plumbing, and electrical. They don't do "partial rehabs" to get the property back to a just-barely rentable condition.

- Steer away from bad neighborhoods. Even though they could make more money off their clients there, they are long-term players with integrity. They aim to make money and do right by their clients, so they shun the risks inherent in neighborhoods with high vacancy rates and criminal activity.

- Have happy existing clients and make testimonials and references available.

- Have property management that's been tested and proven. They have their own personal investment properties with this same management company.

- Sell you properties that are occupied by a qualified tenant. That tenant has been fully screened by the property management company and the supporting paperwork can be made available for your review.

- Provide a homebuyer's warranty on their properties and will go back and fix a repair if something in the renovation process was done incorrectly.

KEY INSIGHT

A good full-service company will sell you properties at discount and with healthy cash flow.

BAD FULL-SERVICE REAL ESTATE GROUPS

The worst thing about bad full-service groups is that they make their money by tricking investors into the market. They are all about the smoke and mirrors, at least until they have your money. The wise investor's response is to focus on due diligence. Commit to finding out if a company merits your business. If you can't decide, walk away.

KEY INSIGHT

Do not let yourself be a foreign statistic for failure. Put investment fundamentals to work. They reduce investment risk and boost profit potential.

In general, the "bad guys":

- Are usually new to the market that they are selling you on. They lack local experience and they will not own any investment property in the area. This is huge! This kind of full-service group does not plan to be in the market for very long. They want to take your money and run, and we call them "fly-by-night" operations.

- Don't allow you to visit their market or discourage you from visiting. They also are wary of supplying the information you request. Questions may be deferred or ignored. This is bad news.

- Are into what the US industry calls "partial rehabs." They may do some cosmetic work inside, but they'll try to tell you that curb appeal doesn't matter in this market. Bigger repairs like the roof, heating/cooling, plumbing, and electrical will rarely be done. If you ask about this strategy, you'll get excuses, not any evidence that the work wasn't required.

- Tend to steer their clients into bad neighborhoods with a long history of drugs, prostitution, and violence. This is how they buy properties so cheaply. No one wants to live there and the banks just want the properties off their books! That makes the price-motivated investor a sitting duck.

- Don't have any existing clients available for references or testimonials. Remember your fundamentals. If a group refuses to answer your questions it's because you won't like the answers. Move on.

- Might tell you they assign little importance to property management because "the tenant will take care of a lot of the details." Others have untested property managers in place. What? You value quality property management and market experience. This group offers neither.

- Claim to be a full-service group but then try to sell you a vacant property. This defies the sound investment fundamentals that might lead you to work with a full-service group.

- Do not offer any warranties or guarantees on the work they have done for you (or say they have done for you). Again, this is not a company you want to work with. Feel free to back away slowly, or run.

20

Analyze Your Deal

It's time to crunch numbers—even "future" numbers. Many beginning investors only analyze the absolute basic expenses when deciding whether a property's income will cover the operating expenses. The most common cry of the soon-to-be-broke investor is, "I found a property and the rent will cover both my mortgage and my taxes!" Sadly, this uninformed view of investing has led these neophytes into some very bad deals.

UNDERSTAND THE PROPERTY'S TRUE POTENTIAL

The key is to be brutally honest about a property's potential. Assess the "true" income that it can deliver (rather than what you hope it will deliver) along with all of the ongoing expenses you'll need to cover with this revenue (much more than just the mortgage and taxes).

This is also true of the costs of closing on a property. Many beginning investors fail to assess the true cost of buying a property, which adds up to much more than just the down payment and legal costs. Sophisticated investors know that there are many additional costs that need to be budgeted out well in advance.

When analyzing a property, remember:

- Crunch: Sophisticated real estate investment comes down to bare-bones number analysis. Take a harsh look at all properties that you will be investing in. Don't ever get caught wearing rose-colored glasses when doing your analysis. (At the end of this Insight, we'll give you a checklist you can use to ensure you are analyzing a property in detail.)

- Be thorough: Leave no details out. Sure it takes an extra few minutes, but this analysis will tell you the truth about the property and save you from getting caught in a bad deal.

CASH-FLOW STATEMENT

Investors need to develop a *pro forma* (forward-looking) cash-flow statement. It's a monthly statement of cash coming in and cash going out to figure out if an investment property can make money. In real estate, cash is king and a healthy amount of positive cash flow is what you're looking for. Setting up a pro forma cash-flow statement will help you to screen your properties and weed out the ones that cannot produce cash flow.

Monthly Pro-Forma Cash-Flow Statement	
INCOME	
Rental Income	
Less Vacancy Allowance	
Gross Effective Income	
EXPENSES	
Property Taxes	
Insurance	
Condo Fees	
Repairs & Maintenance Allowance	
Property Management	
Utilities	
Marketing	
Book Keeping	
Total Expenses	
FINANCING	
1st Mortgage Payment	
Additional Debt Service	
Total Financing	
CASH FLOW	
Cash-Flow	

The reason novice real estate investors find cash-flow statements difficult is that they tend to make three main errors that detract from the statement's validity:

- Not obtaining accurate estimates of rental income

- Not accounting for all expenses

- Not budgeting monthly for annual expenses like insurance and property taxes

On the plus side, every one of those mistakes can be fixed. Investors should commit to a quality in/quality out approach. If you plan to make economic decisions on the basis of your pro forma cash-flow statements, make sure the figures you enter are real. To counter the potential for errors and ensure the cash flow statement has solid information, focus on *cash in* (from rent and other income sources) and *cash out* (from operating and financing expenses).

Cash in: Keep It Real

The first line on the statement is for *gross rental income*. This is the full amount of rent you expect to collect and it's pretty much the most important number to get right. Unfortunately, it's also the number most people get wrong!

To remedy this situation, you need accurate information. Listen to a trusted real estate agent, talk to a property management company, and research other properties for rent. Above all, don't think it's okay to guess at this number. As a foreign investor, you are looking for a good deal in the US market, not a good story about a Canadian getting burned.

Realtors' Data

While market research is essential, never forget where your information is coming from. As an investor, you should be working with realtors who specialize in investment real estate. Work only with agents who actually own and operate investment properties themselves, because these individuals are most likely to have a solid understanding of the rental market and be better able to advise you on what amount of rent to expect.

However, do be on the lookout for real estate agents who inflate prospective rental amounts. They're not necessarily dishonest, but they know investors are more likely to buy a property—and more likely to pay more for that property—when it cash flows. This gives real estate agents an incentive to be very optimistic about rents and overestimate the actual numbers.

Property Managers' Data

The same thing applies to rental data you get from property managers. Property managers can be excellent sources of rental data, especially if they operate large portfolios and rental properties on a daily basis. They will likely have the most accurate rental numbers on the market, but they also have a vested interest in underestimating rents. They tend to be pessimistic and undershoot market rents because they know the property will rent more quickly and more easily if it's under the going market rates. Let's face it, property managers look good when places rent quickly.

The tendency to underestimate a going rental rate will cost the investor much more than it costs the property manager. Say market rent on a property is $1,700 and a property manager advises you to rent it for $1,500. When the property rents quickly, the manager gets the fee faster. In fact, however, both parties will lose. For example, if the property management fee is 10 percent of the rent, a $1,500-a-month property will earn the manager $150 a month instead of $170 a month. Over a year, that's a difference of $240. That same lowball rent estimate costs the investor $200 a month in rent, or $2,400 a year.

One solution is to get rental estimates from real estate agents and property managers and average them. This should help you zero in on an accurate number for the cash-in line.

Compare Numbers

Investors should also look at the rents charged in comparable properties or "comps." This information can be found in the newspaper rentals section, through independent rental surveys, and on rental websites.

Make sure you are looking at properties that are truly comparable: if you have a half-duplex for rent you'd look at other duplexes, not single-family homes or condos. Keeping to similar neighborhoods and amenities will give the most accurate information. Remember, too, that you'll only be able to view "advertised rent." The actual rent after tenant negotiation may differ.

Once you have this data, use the information to set a conservative number for your pro forma cash-flow statement. And remember to be cautious! If your real estate agent says $1,800, your property manager says $1,500, and your average from rental comparables is $1,675, your estimate for cash-flow purposes should be $1,600 to $1,650.

For this example we'll use $1,650. Enter this number in your pro forma cash-flow statement under gross rental income.

Gross Effective Income: Net Rent

Gross effective income, income after you subtract an allowance for vacancy, is "net rent." Stability of income is important in real estate and you have to plan for vacancies before they happen. So, to analyze a deal based on a prospective rent of $1,650, you should subtract a monthly vacancy allowance to account for this by taking the prevailing vacancy rate for an area, or the vacancy rate of the property management company, provided it has a relatively large portfolio. Vacancy statistics are available for virtually every city by searching online. Again, you should be conservative with this estimate.

To calculate that monthly vacancy allowance, multiply the vacancy allowance by the gross rental income, which is then subtracted from the gross rent for a net figure. In this example, with monthly rent of $1,650 a month, and a vacancy rate of 8 percent, the vacancy rate is $1,650 × 8 percent, or $132 for a net rent of $1,518.

Operating Expenses: Decisions are in the Details

Operating expenses are line items that are incurred to run your investment property. Investors who ignore or lowball these numbers are asking for trouble. Operating expenses include the following:

- Property taxes

- Insurance

- Condo fees

- Repairs and maintenance

- Property management

- Utilities

- Marketing expenses

- Accounting and bookkeeping fees

Property Taxes

Property taxes, if not included as part of your mortgage payment, are typically paid annually, but you should be budgeting for them monthly. Find out how much the annual property taxes are when you analyze the property, either from the listing real estate agent or the owner, who should have a copy of last year's tax assessment, or the city tax department. Keep in mind that property taxes are tied to the value of the property, so taxes in the current year could be more than the previous year's assessment if the city tax department determines that values have gone up.

To deal with that uncertainty, you can include a buffer for property tax inflation. If last year's taxes were $1,700, for example, and you believe that property values have come up 10 percent, then add $170 to the estimated property tax amount.

When you have determined the annual property tax estimate, divide it by twelve to get a monthly amount and input that number into your pro forma cash-flow statement. You can create a separate "holding" bank account for these funds, segregated from the regular operating funds, until they are needed at the end of the year. That way your cash flow isn't distorted and it's much more predictable and stable throughout the year.

Insurance

As with property taxes, you should work insurance costs into your pro forma cash-flow statements. Contact an insurance broker and obtain an estimate for insurance, then divide it by twelve to get a monthly amount.

Condo Fees

Investors who own a condo, or a home in a community that has a condo association, also will have monthly fees to pay, which should be included in your pro forma cash-flow statement.

Repairs and Maintenance

Common sense tells you that properties degrade over time, with big items like roofs needing to be replaced every twenty years or so. Your monthly operating expenses should reflect this. Instead of waiting for the roof to go and all of a sudden having to come up with $15,000, you can budget for these expenses in monthly chunks put into a reserve or contingency account. Five percent of gross rent is a good number to put in reserve and you can adjust this upwards for older properties that require more upkeep. Keep in mind that you should be putting aside this money even in months where you don't incur any actual expenses. This way you're running your investment property like a self-contained business, rather than mixing it up with your personal finances.

Property Management

Most property managers for residential properties charge 10 percent of gross rent and some investors try to save this cost by self-managing. You should budget for property management even if you intend to manage the property yourself. What happens if you want to go on a vacation, if you retire, or if you get tired of managing it and want to have the budget to hire a manager? Your time has value and you need to account for it. Making this calculation part of your initial deal analysis ensures the property can support management fees before they're an issue.

Utilities

While the tenant usually pays for power, heat, and phone charges, often water, sewer, and garbage pickup are another matter. The owner also has to pay these charges when the property is vacant. For example, if a property is vacant and you're in an area that is cold, you need to leave the heat on to keep the pipes from freezing. This can be a significant unanticipated expense if you didn't include this in your estimate of operating expenses.

To get accurate information about utilities fees, ask the owner of the property for access to past utilities statements.

Marketing Expenses

Because these expenses affect the accuracy of your cash-flow situation, don't wait until a lease comes up or the property is vacant to budget for things like law signs, online advertising, and print ads. This can be a monthly expense as well and can vary a lot depending on what your marketing strategy is.

Accounting and Bookkeeping Fees

Owning an investment property requires additional tax filing at the end of the year. During the year, you'll also likely want to have a bookkeeper in place to take care of the financials.

Financing

The final component to your pro forma cash-flow statement is financing. Talk to your mortgage broker, who should be able to tell you well in advance of purchasing a property what the expected mortgage payment will be. This figure goes into the first mortgage section of the analysis statement. If you are using additional financing, such as a line of credit, to fund the down payment, or a second mortgage, put this into the Additional Debt Service section.

AND THE FINAL NUMBER IS . . .

With all of these numbers in place, you can determine your monthly cash-flow estimate. To do that, take the gross effective income number and subtract operating expenses and financing. This leaves the expected monthly cash-flow amount. If this number is still positive and healthy after all of your reserves and conservative estimates, then you have yourself a solid acquisition opportunity.

CHECKLIST FOR ENTERING US REAL ESTATE MARKETS

What good are fundamentals you "know about" but don't put into action? Use this checklist to focus your property quest and acquisitions.

I've researched my market. My due diligence includes:

- ❑ People I've talked to
- ❑ Local websites I've researched
  - ○ General websites: city website, chamber of commerce, real estate investors' associations
  - ○ Real estate websites: See Insight 3 for references.

I know what's happening with the five key market drivers.

- ❑ Supply and demand
- ❑ Affordability
- ❑ Desirability
- ❑ Population growth
- ❑ Economic growth

I've got realistic property values from reputable comparable sources.

- ❑ I've talked to at least two real estate agents/brokers.
- ❑ I've got comparables and current or active listings.

I've taken steps to put the right people on my team. Screening includes:

- ❑ Experience/track record
- ❑ Testimonials/references from other investors
- ❑ Information about their own investment properties

I have realistic expectations.

- ❑ I've created my own expectations list.
- ❑ I have a plan of action is those expectations aren't met.

I created a relationship with a top-producing real estate agent/broker, who is:

❑ An investor specialist

❑ Currently investing themselves (versus only having sales experience)

❑ An REO/foreclosure specialist (this is a plus)

My fundamentals value quality property management. My prospective managers know:

❑ Local vacancy rates and average days on market

❑ The size of the portfolio they currently manage and the vacancy rate of that portfolio (many experienced investors want one hundred units, minimum.)

❑ Whether they will handle maintenance in-house or subcontract to outside contractors

My property managers:

❑ Are managing in the submarkets I want to invest in

❑ Have fees within industry norms (industry standards range from 8 to 14 percent of collected rents, plus a placement fee of half a month's rent)

I have considered details and:

❑ Reviewed lease and management agreement contracts and asked a lot of questions

❑ Factored in 25 percent in contingencies of gross rents (management fees, vacancy rate, ongoing maintenance or repairs)

I know my renovation/construction costs.

❑ My budget spreadsheets were based on national average pricing.

❑ I'm getting good information from general contractors.

❑ I know that industry standards for general contractors run 20 to 25 percent margins, plus materials.

❏ I check out sites like homedepot.com to compare prices.

❏ I always get three bids.

I am committed to understanding the tax consequences of my decisions. I understand that I need a cross-country legal and tax specialist to help me:

❏ Determine entity structures

❏ Set up US bank accounts

❏ Make sure I'm not paying more tax than I should

❏ Avoid double taxation

I crunched my numbers. I crunched them again.

❏ I know that I need to keep it real. This is my money.

I visited the market before I bought.

❏ My plane ticket is an investment in my real estate portfolio.

ASK YOURSELF THE TOUGH QUESTIONS

As part of your due diligence, we encourage Canadian investors to look at their deals through the eyes of a skeptic. One of the best ways to do this is to ask the same tough questions you'd ask another investor. Here are some of the questions you might consider, and the answers a smart investor would give.

Q. Are you going to allow someone to sell you a property just because it's a cheap price and has the potential for high rent returns?

A. No! I'm going to look at what the overall market is like in that area. I'll find out what this neighborhood is like in particular. I will investigate the property's condition to make sure it's worth renovating.

Q. Are you going to make an emotional decision because the house is new and pretty?

A. Again, no. I want to know if there is rental demand, if there's cash flow and if the market has strong fundamentals.

Q. Are you about to let the person who's selling you a fixer-upper quote on the property upgrade and tell you what work is needed?

A. No way! I do my own research. (And I don't ask the barber if I need a haircut, either!)

Q. Are you going to buy a house now and find property management later?

A. No. I've done the opposite. Money follows management. I've got a property manager who knows my market and can meet my expectations.

Q. Have you been crunching the numbers and building your team even before you've acquired a deal?

A. Yes, because that's how smart investors work.

KNOW HOW TO CRUNCH THE NUMBERS THAT COUNT

A good deal is only a good deal if the numbers work! Once you know your exit strategy, plug in the numbers to see if a prospective deal makes sense.

Buy and Hold

purchase price + closing costs + initial repairs = total investment

rents − debt service (mortgage, taxes, insurance) − 25 percent gross rents (contingency for repairs management & vacancy) = monthly cash flow

Fix and Flip

purchase price + closings + initial repairs = total investment

resale price − purchase price − repair costs − closing costs (both on purchase and resale) − holding costs (any interest, fees paid on money that funded the deal) − real estate commissions = profit

RENOVATIONS AND MANAGEMENT

21 Work Smartly with Contractors and Subcontractors

If you buy US residential real estate property that needs any kind of renovation or repair, you will need to work with contractors and subcontractors. When it comes to making money from a residential real estate investment, this is one area where a significant amount of money can be made or lost very easily. Never presume you can't learn something new about the investor/contractor relationship or be reminded about something you could be doing better.

Having a positive attitude is important. A good working relationship with your contractor will keep your renovation and repair projects on time and on budget. The right attitude is also an essential part of making sure you finish with a quality product. But this relationship is a two-way street. Time, money, and quality can be compromised by a won't-do attitude, putting your investment at risk, and quickly turning a good deal into a bad one.

KEY INSIGHT

Your contractor needs to have a positive attitude, too! Where time, money, or quality considerations aren't meeting your expectations, rethink your choice of contractor. When those three expectations are met, you probably have a contractor with the right attitude and by default you'll get a great job. If the relationship's working, let your contractor know. If the relationship's not working, cut your losses.

FIVE COMMON-SENSE RULES

These five common-sense rules in dealing with contractors and subcontractors are designed to keep a project on time and on budget so that a quality job or product improves your investment. Think about them and always remember: in the business world, as in life, common sense isn't all that common. People who try to circumvent these five rules are asking for a lot of unnecessary headaches.

1. Assume the Role of the Pack Leader

Recognize that being the pack leader does not mean showing up to the job site and screaming or being overly aggressive about what you want done (and when you want it done). It does mean, however, that you need to deal with situations as soon as you can when you see, or even suspect, that any of your expectations are not being met.

Communicate Respectfully

Communicate with contractors about things that are positive and that are negative—be calm, yet assertive. When things look great on the job, offer praise. When things are not being done correctly on the job, ask for a resolution.

When you develop this kind of honest communication with your general contractors, they will understand that any questions you ask are fair in the context of your relationship with them. And what kind of relationship is it? It's business, all business.

The way you communicate with your general contractors will affect how those individuals manage and communicate with their subs and labor on the job. That is a definite bonus and it should be good news to your bottom line and to the bottom line of the general contractor as well. In the end, clear expectations of everyone involved in a property upgrade increases the likelihood that everyone will make money.

Permits

As pack leader, you also must take responsibility for making sure the proper permits are pulled when necessary and on all jobs. City or county inspectors may fine you and the general contractor if you're caught doing work without a permit. As the property owner, you could also find yourself having to pay to "undo" that work. In a competitive renovation and rehab market, you must also consider that the contractors you didn't hire may have a vested interest in sinking your investment ship.

When work has a permit, a city or county inspector will come out and give a final inspection. They will pass or fail the work that's been done, giving you a valuable guarantee that the work has been done correctly.

In Part 5, you'll get a better look at why real estate investors working in the United States must consider how every aspect of their operation reinforces or weakens their comprehensive asset protection plan. From this perspective, a city or county work permit is one more investment fundamental—one more way to show a potential litigant that you have done your due diligence.

2. Communicate. Communicate. Communicate. And Then Get it in Writing

Bad things happen when people do not take the time to make sure that everyone involved with a renovation or repair project knows what is expected of them. Communication is key. Make it a point to be redundant. Your end goal is to make sure your contractor knows exactly what you expect on each and every job.

You also want to make sure you have one point of contact, one go-to person, for each job. This is usually the general contractor, since he's the one you're paying. A single point of contact helps avoid any breakdowns in communication.

Always get what you want in writing, too. This is important even if you have worked with the same contractor for many years. Skip the guesswork and ensure details are written down. Begin each project with a formal proposal or bid and make sure the scope of the work that you expect to be done is recorded and can be reviewed.

Never leave the details to a contractor's discretion. No two sets of eyes see a job the same way and you do not want to be disappointed when someone guesses what you wanted and gets it wrong.

KEY INSIGHT

Avoid the complications and potential costs of a he said/she said situation. A written scope of work is essential. It can be used to track work done and, where necessary, job amendments.

---

3. Pay What the Job is Worth

Investors who try to nickel-and-dime their contractors will live to pay the piper, as this is a save-now-and-pay-later strategy that will bite you in the bank account! Worse yet, this approach works both ways: if you try to cut corners on your contractors and their bids, it is guaranteed they will also cut corners that affect the quality of your job.

When it comes to budgets and estimates, be proactive and realistic. If you have done your cost estimates and you know it's a $25,000 job, don't expect to get it done for $18,000. Real estate investors who think they've gotten away with a lowball contract should be especially wary of what's really going on. Are you prepared to pay a stingy price today in return for having to pay to fix the problem later? Because that's what will happen after a tenant moves in and finds the problem or when you may have to make improvements or cut your asking price before you can sell it.

If you are in the business of fixing up properties to operate as investments, you need to find quality contractors you can work with. But they need to be able to work with you, too. It is more efficient, economical, and effective to get a job done right the first time.

KEY INSIGHT

Smart real estate investors build sustainable relationships with general contractors and subcontractors who do quality work. If you treat them the way you want to be treated, they will reward you by helping you make money. Always remember that, just like you, your contractors have bills and families to feed. The more turnover you have with contractors and the more contractors you have to hire and fire, the less time you spend marketing your real estate properties. That's going to cost you.

---

4. Know What Volume can Buy You

The property upgrade market in the United States offers some good opportunities for price discounts based on volume. The more volume you do with a vendor or associate, the better pricing you can and should expect on your jobs.

The industry standard is 25-percent profit margins for general contractors in the single-family home renovation or rehab niche. Once you get to a point where you are doing more than five rehabs at a time, you should start to negotiate pricing discounts with the general contractors you are working with on those jobs.

Your goal is not to take advantage of a contractor, but to give both of you an opportunity to realize discounts for volume buys in materials, for example. Always shop for deals and ask your general contractor to do the same. In reality, no one cares about your money the way you do. But talking about the discounts you've come across is a good way to remind your contractor that you're watching the market and you expect him to do the same. In the end, a couple of hundred dollars saved on each job adds up very quickly when your volume increases.

One savvy investor says he keeps a close eye on the industry and is confident that a 12 to 15-percent profit margin is fair in the context of how much work he gives his general contractors and their subs. In fact, he talks about this openly with all of his general contractors and they agree with his position. What does this look like in the context of a job? If the contractor is looking at $10,000 in materials, the investor figures the bid should come in at around $11,500 for the total job, including materials, permits, and labor.

He says his contractor would rather make a little less on each job but know he is guaranteed more work in the future as long as the investor's expectations are met on the current job—again, demonstrating the importance of relationships.

This kind of open communication acknowledges that the investor knows he's not the only one negotiating costs. He negotiates costs with the general contractors who do volume work for his business, but he knows they also are negotiating with their suppliers. In the end, it's the trickle-down theory at work and all parties need to seek win-win relationships.

5. Without Options, You Have No Power, So Always Get Three Bids on Every Job

We cannot stress this enough. The basic premise is simple: with options, you can bargain from a position of power; without options, you have nothing with which to negotiate!

Apply this concept to the bid process and you can see why it is imperative to always get three bids on any major rehab you plan to undertake. But use common sense—when you need a $30-light replaced on a rental property, the process of seeking three bids is neither efficient nor effective. Your time is also valuable and the work you have to do to save $5 on a $30-light is not worth it.

As a general rule, have your property manager seek three bids on any job over $250 to $300, and have that requirement stipulated in writing in the management agreement.

The key point here is that any significant property repair or upgrade should be shopped around for pricing. This also helps you maintain a healthy spirit of competition among your general contractors.

In the end, three bids are always better than two, but remember to schedule your contractor bid meetings so that you don't have three general contractors pull up at your front door at the same time.

Don't Confuse Apples with Oranges

When you are comparing bids, check the quality of materials each general contractor plans to use. A lowball price is no good to you if it is based on substandard materials. This is a particular concern if you are getting bids on one of the big four renovation items addressed in Insight 24.

The nuance-filled bid process is one area where your relationship with quality contractors can make or break your investment deal, so ask lots of questions. For example, if one contractor recommends a 2.5-ton air conditioning system with no warranty and another bid features a 3-ton system with a warranty, you can expect a bid price difference. If there isn't one, find out why.

KEY INSIGHT

The cheapest bid is not always the way to go. Always check references from prior jobs and take the time to inspect the previous work of a general contractor who's bidding on your job if he or she has never worked for you before. You can also check county records or visit the Better Business Bureau website (www.bbb.org) to see if the general contractor has any complaints against him or her from previous clients.

22

Weigh Reno Must-Haves with Nice-to-Haves

You can move walls, paint, upgrade the flooring, enhance curb appeal, and make sure the HVAC (heating and air conditioning), roof, plumbing, and electrical systems are in dependable working order, but that might not seal the deal. Industry research shows that when it comes to making a sale or signing a rental contract, buyers and renters are predisposed to take a special look at two places where they plan on spending a great deal of time: the kitchen and the bathrooms.

Other than replacing or repairing the "big four," which is the topic of Insight 24, the real estate investor likely will spend most of the money in his or her budget on the kitchen. And that strategy is a good one. You'll sell or rent a house quickly if you've properly rehabbed the kitchen.

THE KITCHEN: PUT THE THREE E'S TO WORK

Every renovation project must be efficient, effective, and economical. These *three E's* are even more important when you are renovating a house as a business investment, since every extra day a house spends on the market has the potential to cost you money.

But where do you begin with a kitchen remodel? New and updated flooring (tile or hardwood), paint, and lights or chandeliers are a must for every kitchen remodel. In terms of efficiency and knowing where to start, these are your top picks. Zeroing in on these items also makes your project more effective, since these are among the first things a potential buyer or renter will notice.

Once you have a plan to improve those items, you have to decide whether you are going to demolish the cabinets and countertops or refurbish the existing materials. If you're not careful, cabinets and countertops can wreak serious havoc on your rehab budget.

Your Exit Strategy Defines Your Actions

Approach this part of the project with care—and good advice. Many older cabinets can be salvaged and refurbished to look new, but a cabinet and counter rehab is one area where your knowledge of your potential buyer must come into play.

Experienced investors in the US foreclosure market say that if their exit strategy is to buy and hold the property for long-term appreciation and current cash flow and they don't need to gut and replace the whole kitchen, they always make sure the property goes onto the rental market with the cabinets freshly repainted and all hardware and handles replaced with new product. They also will lay new granite tile over the existing dated countertops and have a new backsplash installed.

KEY INSIGHT

Granite tile and new backsplashes are an investment in fewer future maintenance hassles.

Where experienced investors plan to flip a property, usually to a first-time homebuyer as a retail sale of a foreclosed-and-rehabbed property, they will spend considerably more time and money. Here, they will replace the existing cabinets and counters with new cabinets and new solid-surface granite countertops and a stone backsplash.

They will also install new stainless steel appliances, including a stove with a hood vent/exhaust fan, a fridge, and a dishwasher. If the property is to be rented out, they will still replace old appliances (unless they are clean and relatively new), but will opt for a brand new white stove and fridge (white appliances look great and are more cost effective than the stainless steel options). In a rental property, they'll look at whether the niche market and price point demand a dishwasher.

KEY INSIGHT

Pay keen attention to what is considered a "standard product" in the market you're entering. You will need to match or slightly upgrade your product to be competitive, but there may be nothing to be gained from top-end additions. In many rental markets, a dishwasher is an extra, not a must-have.

What About the Floor Plan?

In addition to considering the cabinets, countertops, and appliances, investors must look at whether they can improve a kitchen floor plan. An open floor plan kitchen is very desirable in contemporary markets and US real estate insiders say they will remove an existing wall to open a kitchen up and make it appear bigger.

This can be a significant budget item if the wall you want to move is weight-bearing (structural). In that case, you cannot remove the entire wall because it is supporting the weight and integrity of the roof. But you can partially open this wall with a pass-through arch or by creating a custom bar top. These can increase the kitchen's functionality and improve the space's aesthetics, often by adding the illusion of more space.

On projects where you do add a bar or an extra sitting area, always match the granite countertops to the bar top that you add. That might seem like a minor detail, but when these two counters do not match, it detracts from the overall impact of the changes you've made.

Let the Light in

Also look for ways to add natural light to a kitchen. Where there is a double sliding glass door or an exterior door in or near the kitchen, experts say it's a good idea to replace the sliders with new French doors or replace the exterior door with a glass door.

Always consider replacing outdated kitchen windows with new windows. Where possible, it also makes sense to add an extra window to an existing wall.

KEY INSIGHT

Anytime you add more natural light to an interior space, you make the space brighter and you make it appear larger. Since kitchens are a flashpoint for a rehab's success or failure, look for ways to augment the space's attractiveness with natural light.

THE BATHROOM

When it comes to must-have renovations, bathrooms are right behind kitchens in terms of priority. Potential buyers and renters will check out a home's bathrooms right after they've assessed the kitchen. Investors should expect a good portion of their renovation budget to be spent on the bathrooms and they will need to make their choices based on what is efficient, effective, and economical in terms of their exit strategy.

One of the first things you must consider when buying a foreclosure or rehab project is the number of bathrooms. Experienced US investors say they will not buy a foreclosure or rehab project unless it has at least one full bath and one half-bath they can easily convert into a full second bathroom for marketability.

While market demographics must be considered, think of the number of bathrooms as a key selling and renting feature in every market. A three-bedroom, two-bathroom home is always more desirable than a three-bedroom home with a half-bath or a three-bedroom home with one bath. A lot of the foreclosures a colleague of ours buys in the US have three bedrooms with one bath or three bedrooms with one and a half baths. In both cases, he converts the properties to two full baths.

Finding the space to add a bathroom is easier than you might think. Many floor plans already have a half-bath, usually in the common space or a hallway. Adding a shower/tub unit to the half-bath is a relatively easy conversion because the plumbing is already in place.

KEY INSIGHT

The lack of a second bathroom in a property can stop a real estate investment deal in its tracks. If there is no space to add an extra bathroom, the property had better have some other great features before you jump in and buy. Always think functionality. Will the people who live there need a second bathroom? If it's a three-bedroom home, the answer is pretty obvious.

When it comes to adding a bathroom, a little creativity goes a long way. For example, if the existing floor plan is a three-bedroom, one-and-a-half bath arrangement and the half-bath is in the master suite, think about moving a wall to make the master bath into a full bath. You might lose some closet space—but your buyer or renter won't notice because they'll be so happy to have the extra bathroom!

Your goal as an investor is to think about what will quickly sell the home. There is no magic formula, but your buyers and renters will be looking at functionality. And when it comes to adding an extra bathroom, that functionality is a common-sense proposition.

KEY INSIGHT

Every remodeling project should be efficient, effective, and economical. When you're deciding which budget items to keep or toss, think about your market and what will really sell a home to a buyer or renter. Kitchen and bathroom makeovers are essential.

23

Dial Up the Intellect (Dial Down the Emotions)

There is a little saying in the real estate investment business: check your emotions at the door. One of the cardinal errors one sees real estate investors making time and again is unconsciously bringing emotion into the decision-making process when they are deciding what they need to do to buy or sell a property. We can guarantee you that those who bring emotions into investment decisions will make poor decisions, and will pay dearly for that mistake.

To be clear, we are not talking about restraining your enthusiasm for your work! Enthusiasm is great and people should be enthusiastic about investing in US residential real estate. When we recommend investors be consciously emotional, we are referring to the need to be crystal clear that the decisions you make regarding improvements to an investment property should never be confused with the decisions you might make about upgrading a personal residence. (This is a great place to review Insight 22, about recognizing the differences between a must-have renovation and a nice-to-have renovation.)

EMOTION VERSUS PASSION

Some real estate investors struggle with the "working difference" between emotion and passion.

Being genuinely enthusiastic about real estate investing means you leave a deal talking about the next one. You take a healthy pride in a job well done, a deal well executed. When things go well, you celebrate the fundamentals of your investment system and move on. When things go astray, you step up to the plate, deal with the problems and move on.

When emotions get in the way of a sound investment decision, an investor will find himself sentimentally caught up in the details of a deal. You will have very strong feelings about why certain aspects of the deal will work and those feelings will make you second-guess the need to check your fundamentals. When problems arise after your emotional investment decision, you will be disappointed and will want to look for someone else to blame. Here are some examples of what emotional investing might look like in action:

- A naïve investor is so star-struck by a master bathroom and powder room retrofit that she misses asking important questions about the overall plumbing. She mistakenly credits the upgrade in her offering price and, after the deal is complete, finds herself financially responsible for a major retrofit of the property's copper pipes.

- An investor who's also renting falls in love with a foreclosure property he tours. (This can be an especially costly mistake for foreign investors who let their appreciation for sun and palm trees get in the way of their investment fundamentals.) Because he thinks he can picture himself living in a particular neighborhood and on a particular street, he ignores the reality of that neighborhood's rental pool demographic. He pays more than he should and can't find a renter for a monthly rate that will make his bad deal work.

- An investor gets so excited about a discounted price that he throws caution to the wind and makes a cash deal. It turns out that the property needs major work. The neighborhood is rife with crime and the only people who want to rent a home there are the people who won't pay the rent! In return for ignoring his real estate foreclosure investment fundamentals, this investor is impaled on a very sharp financial hook. He feels as though he was lied to. In reality, he forgot to look for the truth.

HOW MUCH TO SPEND

One of the first things to remember is that financial decisions about how to upgrade a property range from inexpensive to over-the-top. You can watch the Home and Garden TV (HGTV) network to get ideas for renovations, which are called "rehabs" in the United States, but be aware that many of the decisions to be made are highly subjective, especially when you're improving a single-family home.

There are TV shows, for example, where a general contractor spends $25,000 to landscape a front yard. These yards look great, but you can also remodel entire homes, including the landscape, for the same amount of money or less. Similarly, Italian marble countertops, imported French doors, limited-edition Swiss cabinets, and SubZero stainless appliances would look fabulous in a $100,000 rental home. But your choices should be driven by the financial reality of what you are trying to do. While you easily could spend $25,000 upgrading just a kitchen, you can also complete a functional kitchen and get an entire home ready for quality tenants to move in for the same $25,000 budget. Which option will help you make money? That is what you need to be enthusiastic about!

EXIT STRATEGY

To keep emotions out of the equation, always keep in mind your exit strategy (sale or rental) and the price point in the market you are competing with. This will help you keep your upgrades in line. You also need to know the type of materials that are standard for that product or neighborhood. Again, this will help you keep your project's finances under control.

If you're still not sure about the differences between emotional decision-making and investing with passion, consider this. As a real estate investor, your goal should be to take one of the worst homes on the block and make it the best on that block every time. You want a functional, newly remodeled home with great curb appeal that someone in your target market will be thrilled to move into and take care of. Always remember, however, that your investments are not homes you would necessarily move into.

KEY INSIGHT

Nothing increases enthusiasm for investing like staying on budget for a renovation or repair. Sure, you can install a high-end chic kitchen and sell a property more quickly, but if you don't make money on the deal you haven't met your investment goal.

LOOK AND ASK AROUND

Experienced investors know it's okay to talk to general contractors and real estate professionals about what they should and should not do with a property upgrade. New investors should adopt the same strategy. Remember when we talked about the win-win scenario you want to achieve with your contractors so everyone makes some money? (See Insight 21 for a refresher.) Rest assured that experienced contractors and real estate agents put the same principle to work in their businesses. In other words, they know that a good real estate investor can help them make money, too.

24 Do the Big Four Renos on a Rental Property—Now

Now that we've talked a bit about nice-to-haves versus must-haves, let's zero in the *big four renos*: heating and cooling systems, roofs, plumbing, and electrical. Experienced real estate investors will confirm: you can either do the big four right away or pay a lot more to have them done later.

Before we get into the specifics of the big four, let's quickly review the pay now/pay later rule of thumb, because it has obvious implications for virtually every aspect of the renovation process. What you need to think about here is the idea that more than money is at stake. As Warren Buffett said:

> *"It takes twenty years to build a reputation and five minutes to lose it. If you think about that, you will do things differently."*

The renovation decisions you make will have long-term effects on your investment. Those who go for the quick fix when doing a property rehab are playing with fire. The quick fix may lead to a quick buck early in your investment career, but the investors, brokers, contractors, lenders, and property buyers you need to make your real estate investment ventures a success over the long term will not stick with your team if you've got a reputation for sacrificing quality for speed. Good news travels fast. Bad news travels faster.

MAKE SUSTAINABILITY A FUNDAMENTAL PRIORITY

Sustainability should always be the underlying fundamental when making decisions about how to handle a renovation. Whether your exit strategy is selling or a long-term buy-and-hold rental property, always do what needs to be done up front to get the job done right.

And never forget what's really at stake. If you cut corners on the initial property upgrade, you will either have an upset buyer or renter, a property that sits unsold or unrented, a ruined reputation, or an unhealthy combination of all of these things.

KEY INSIGHT

Be honest about what a property needs. If you are buying bank foreclosures at deep discounts, you can expect that property will need a complete reno nearly 100 percent of the time. Factor that knowledge into your business strategy.

THE BIG FOUR

After undertaking hundreds of renos that were resold or held in rental portfolios, real estate renovation insiders emphasize that investors in the US foreclosure market have got to zero in on the big four: replacing or repairing the property's heating and cooling systems, roof, plumbing, and electrical systems virtually every time you add a new foreclosure property to your portfolio.

If you have ever owned or rented a home, you probably already know that these four items are the source of most of the problem calls from or to your property manager, landlord, or tenant. This happens because a lot of investors will try to deal with the big four by doing only minimal repairs, taking a band-aid approach because their initial renovation and repair budget did not make these four areas a priority, or they spent too much on the property itself and are now trying to squeeze a profit from a bad deal.

Always remember what's really at stake: your reputation and potentially your relationships with members of your investment team. While the United States is undoubtedly a big market, chances are you will be concentrating your investments in particular market niches, within specific geographic areas, so the reputation you build is important.

KEY INSIGHT

Avoid being shocked by big four repairs and replacements by factoring these costs into your investment plan up front. Then learn to take quick responsibility for your mistakes. If you've missed something in your initial renovation budget, deal with the mistake and accept that it will cost you. Savvy investors know they make their money when they buy, so as long as you buy at the right price (with the right reno budget figures included), a renovation surprise should not consume your entire profit because it will probably be a cosmetic item, instead of something from the big four list.

Heating and Cooling Systems

In many parts of Canada, residents can enjoy summer temperatures without ever feeling the need for an air conditioner. In Nevada, Arizona, Florida, and California, states with some of the best real estate investment opportunities in the United States, residential air conditioning is a fact of life!

In America, heating and cooling systems have an average life span of ten to twelve years. Be realistic. If you are buying a property that's a bank foreclosure, it's likely the system was not properly maintained by the property's previous owner or resident. One of the biggest problems is also painfully simple to solve: research shows tenants and property owners do not change out air filters every ninety to 120 days, the typical recommended time span, depending on the system. Filters literally cost only $2 to $5, but because the air handler is in a closet (out of sight, out of mind), they are rarely changed and often are not replaced for years. This basic lack of maintenance will destroy a system very quickly and can lead to a situation where the whole system must be replaced far earlier than its expected life span.

Given the potential for this expense to cut into his profit margins, an experienced real estate investor follows a specific rule in his approach to the heating and cooling systems. When he buys a property that needs to be rehabbed and the heating and cooling system doesn't have at least five years of life left (the manufacture date is usually on the handler and condenser), he will plan to replace the entire system and include that cost in his bid. If the system has five years of life left, he will, at minimum, plan to have the air handler and the condenser cleaned and serviced. He wants to make sure the system is working properly before he markets the home.

KEY INSIGHT

If you are going to buy and hold rental property, have your general contractor place six new filters in the house and let your tenant know it is their responsibility to change out the filter every three months. Write that into your rental agreement with the tenants.

Roofs

North and south of the Canada–US border, roofs are generally the most expensive item to replace in a typical investment property rehab. Apply the same five-year life span rule used with the heating and cooling system to the roof: if the existing roof doesn't have at least five years of life left and shows signs of water damage on the interior ceilings, replace the entire roof.

If your roofer tells you the roof has five years of life left, have him inspect and seal or patch as necessary. In this scenario, always get a two-year roof certification, which will either guarantee his work or guarantee that the roof will not leak for two years.

KEY INSIGHT

A typical roof certificate, which certifies the usual twenty-five-year shingle roof, will cost you approximately $250. Manufacturers generally warrant the material for the life of the shingle and the roofer will warrant the labor for two years.

Plumbing

Many foreclosed homes, especially if they are thirty years old or older, will have the original copper plumbing throughout the house. Given the degradation that can occur to these pipes, these homes will require a complete re-plumb of the hot and cold lines. Ignore this issue and you will pay later: ongoing plumbing issues are probably the number one expense in rental property.

To alleviate this expense, always factor in a complete house re-plumb during the initial renovation. This entails removing all of the original copper lines in the kitchen, baths, and utility rooms, and replacing them with CPVC. This is a plastic plumbing material that is non-porous and does not corrode or rust like copper, and is the material used in all new construction homes in the United States.

KEY INSIGHT

If you plan to invest in the US market, and especially the foreclosure market, make plumbing retrofits a priority. If that doesn't work with the deal you're trying to make, you've got the wrong deal.

Electrical Systems

Again, this fundamental often applies to investment properties on both sides of the border, so it's nothing new to Canadians. Generally speaking, in any home that is thirty-plus years old that has been purchased as a bank foreclosure, you can expect to have electrical issues because the system may not be up to code.

In some states, a 100-amp service was normal in homes built thirty years ago when the typical home did not consume nearly as much energy as a contemporary household (there may not even have been dishwashers and washer/dryers, let alone microwaves and large heating and cooling systems). To meet the electrical needs of the contemporary home in the United States, you will need to provide a minimum 150-amp panel service. Make sure your investment team includes an electrician who can help you with budgets.

If the US homes you are looking to buy were built before the 1930s, knob and tube wiring may also be a significant rehab issue. Comprised of insulated copper conductors, protective porcelain insulating tubes and nailed-down porcelain knob insulators, these systems have been replaced by power cables. Because of the threat of fire, knob and tube wiring is considered an insurance issue, and is permitted under the National Electrical Code in only a few very specific situations.

Knowledgeable industry insiders say that if you buy and flip or rent a renovated home in the United States, you should upgrade the panel to a 200-amp service if the home is 1,200 square feet or more. This is a safety issue. You also need to make sure that all outlets within three feet of a water source (for example, kitchen and bathroom sinks) are grounded with GFI (ground fault interrupter) outlets. Any inspector will require this to pass code requirements. Remember, pay now or pay later. It's your choice.

25

Get Everything in Writing

The idea that you should always work with written contracts is nothing more than old-fashioned common sense. However, it is still amazing how many property renovations are completed (and property sales performed!) without a clear, legal written contract signed by both parties. Neglecting a proper contract is a bad idea when you are doing all of your real estate business in your home city and your home country. It's a *very* bad idea when you decide, as a Canadian, to start investing in US property. If you are doing renovation business in the United States without a signed contract, you're putting your whole real estate portfolio at risk.

In addition to having a written contract for the scope of work you want performed, you must carry proper insurance. If you own a property where people have been hired to undertake repairs and renovations, you are responsible for what happens to them when they are on your property. You need property, disability, and liability insurance as soon as you own that property. Working in the land of the litigious, you also need to an umbrella policy to cover all of the what-ifs involved with the business of renting property to others. The link between insurance and asset protection is an essential part of your business. Remember: 95 percent of lawsuits worldwide are filed in the United States.

This tendency to skip a written contract seems to happen more often when the same homeowners/investors continually hire the same contractors to renovate their properties. The only way this scenario can have a happy ending is if both parties verbally agree on all the details of a project, after which every one of those details is realized. That means complete agreement on the scope of work, the type of materials to be used, the timelines from start to finish, and the price. Without a written contract, you can only hope the project comes in on time, is on budget, and ends with the quality finished product you were expecting. At this point, there's not much you can do about project deficiencies!

If you're reading this and you've had a project with no written contract go well, you are very lucky. If you think this is a good way to continue to do business, you are delusional.

THE SIX GOLDEN RULES OF THE WRITTEN CONTRACT

Rather than focus on the many ways a handshake deal can go wrong, let's talk about what the smart real estate investor should do when embarking on a repair or renovation project. Following are the six golden rules of the written contract.

1. Make Sure the Contract Is Signed and Dated and Both Parties Have Copies

What's the fastest way to add value to a written contract in the United States? Make sure it is signed and dated by both parties and that both parties have a copy for their records. In the US, if both parties do not have a signed and dated written contract, the contract is null and void.

2. Include a Detailed Scope of Work

The contract must detail the scope of work, the legal address of where the work is to be performed, and the list of required permits.

Steer clear of contractors who tell you to save money by skipping the permit process. As the owner of the property, you can be fined by city or county inspectors for doing work without a permit. If you follow the process correctly, a city inspector will inspect the finished work and give you a pass or fail on the project. This is an excellent way for you to get a guarantee that work was done correctly. From an asset protection perspective, a permit (and that final inspection report) is important proof of your due diligence.

3. Be Specific About the Payment Schedule and Detail Prices Line By Line

The written contract must cover questions such as these: How much money does the contractor require up front? When are subsequent payments due?

If changes to the project scope force changes to the project price (e.g., higher labor costs) you and the general contractor can use the written contract to negotiate how those issues will be handled.

4. Always Detail the Materials to be Used

Your goal here is to be as specific as possible, so always include the manufacturer, size, and type of the product or materials you want the contractor to use, as well as a price list. A detailed list of materials and products provides an important check-and-balance against a contractor who might try to substitute cheaper products. Since a lot of manufacturers market products at a wide variety of price points, you want to be specific about the materials and products you are expecting to be used or installed.

If prices or materials change, you and the general contractor can refer to this part of the contract to guide a conversation about how this will be managed.

5. Stipulate Project Timelines and Penalties

The completion date of a property rehab will have a significant impact on your business plan. It can dictate when a property can go on the market for resale or rental, thus affecting how and when you cover your financing. If a project completion deadline is missed, the contract should stipulate a clear penalty schedule. This keeps your contractor honest. He may have another project that needs his attention, but a penalty clause ensures that it is in his best interest to complete your job on time.

6. Keep Copies of Your General Contractor's Business Documents

Fly-by-night contractors and tradespeople are a dime a dozen in up-and-down real estate markets, on both sides of the border. If there's money to be made, there are crooks out to make it! For this reason, and the fact it offers some guarantee of quality workmanship, Canadians entering the US real estate investment market should always hire reputable contractors with current state licenses, proof of disability and liability insurance, and valid workman's compensation coverage.

The more you work in the US business environment, the more you will appreciate how best practices like this can keep your business on track while reducing your exposure to lawsuits.

Keep copies of all the contractor documents we've noted. If a general contractor bidding on your project balks at this request, don't consider his bid as one of the three bids you need to get. Move on to a company that is prepared to demonstrate a higher level of professionalism. Keeping copies of the contractor's state licence, proof of disability and liability insurance, and workman's compensation documents will help protect you or your company from liability.

HOW TO HANDLE CONTRACT CHANGES

If "get it in writing" is rule number one about the rehab contract, rule number two is "expect contract edits."

When questions about a contract arise or you need to clarify the language used, discuss the issue with your general contractor. When you agree on changes, make notes to the original contract and initial the changes. If there are issues or questions you can't agree on, do not hesitate to employ a real estate lawyer to review the contract to ensure you are getting in writing exactly what you expect.

KEY INSIGHT

If this written contract process is new to you, seek legal advice before you sign a contract. This is also a good thing to do before you sign a particularly complicated contract. From a business perspective, it makes no sense to try to save a few hundred dollars in legal fees if it leaves you and your company exposed to a legal dispute that could cost tens of thousands of dollars on a major property renovation that wasn't completed to your liking.

KEEP IT SIMPLE

Some people who are new to the real estate investment industry may be tempted to view a written contract as an unnecessary complication. They are confused. In the end, any property rehab on a single-family home, which is the key market we're talking about in this book, really comes down to a structure that's four walls and a roof. We don't want to complicate that. But it will complicate itself very quickly if you, as the investor, are not willing and able to clarify exactly what you want done. The simplest way to make sure you get what you want—and what you pay for—is to decide what you want and then put it in writing.

26 Curb Appeal: You've Got Seven Seconds to Impress Me

Research shows that it takes people just seven seconds to make up their minds about the people they date and the folks they plan to hire. Real estate investors should expect their resale and rental properties to elicit the same gut reactions from prospective buyers and renters pulling up to the front sidewalk. They will tend to like or loathe a place almost immediately (and may not even be able to articulate why they feel the way they do).

The raw potency of that initial reaction aside, we know that the key features of a home, from price to location, the number of bedrooms and bathrooms, and the layout of a kitchen, can and will make a difference to motivated buyers and renters. However, never assume that the wisdom of the sober second-thought experience is a license to ignore the significant dollar value connected to that age-old notion of curb appeal.

And let's be brutally honest. There are real estate investors who believe curb appeal is so subjective it can't possibly matter, but we're here to tell you that it does matter. And it matters in every neighborhood and at every price point in the real estate market.

Indeed, if kitchens and bathrooms are requirements of a successful property rehab project, then boosting a home's curb appeal is the icing on the renovation cake. That's why successful real estate investors, including those working in the US foreclosure market, recognize that it's their job to take the worst-looking house on the block and make it the best. (It's also why so many real estate TV shows are dedicated to curb appeal and landscaping.)

KEY INSIGHT

Not every investor "gets" curb appeal. If you can't look at the yard and the exterior of a home and see how you can improve it to encourage a buyer or renter, get help. This is a business decision, especially in markets where several homes on the same street may be for sale or rent. So keep your eye on the prize. Your goal as an investor is to move property as quickly as you can. Every time a buyer or renter chooses a neighboring property, it costs you money.

AN EXTERIOR MAKEOVER

Think beauty is skin deep? Get over it. When it comes to curb appeal, you've got to acknowledge the value of the first impression. In earlier Insights in this book, we talked about what it's like to find yourself in a "bad" neighborhood in the United States. We also know that some really good American neighborhoods have been plagued by foreclosures. Make sure the exterior view of your investment property leaves buyers and renters curious to see the inside of your property.

Always remember that the need to upgrade an investment property's curb appeal holds true regardless of whether you intend to flip or rent the newly rehabbed home. Here are five specific things to keep in mind with a curb appeal upgrade.

1. Make Sure the Property Looks Well Maintained

If you're an investor, you want to make smart decisions, not emotional ones. The inverse is true with your approach to using curb appeal to attract buyers and renters. Here, the investor wants prospective buyers and renters to have an emotional reaction to their first impression of a property. They are looking at your investment because they want a home. Your curb appeal goal is to make them want to live there.

At its most basic level, this means making sure the property looks like it's well maintained. Fix or remove broken fences. Trim the lawn and hedges, and remove weeds from flower gardens and planters. Repair broken steps and clear away all refuse.

2. Give It Some Fresh Paint

It's tempting to think you need to spend all of your renovation money on the interior because that's where your buyers or renters will be spending their time. But if you want a home to rent or sell fast, you've got to look at fresh paint for the exterior.

A fresh coat of paint is the best bang for your buck after cleaning up the yard. A neutral palette is a good investment for the main part of the house. (Think contemporary, but classic.) Trim, fascia, shutters, and the front door may be treated to a contrasting color that "pops" for visual effect.

If the house is made of brick, pressure wash the exterior and only paint the trim, fascia, shutters, and any exterior doors.

3. Improve the Landscape

Nothing says "improved curb appeal" in a competitive market like improving the landscape. Unfortunately, this is the one area most frequently ignored by investors. That's a shame, since unless there is a whole lot of tree trimming to do, you can probably improve the landscape for less than $1,000.

If you're not sure where to start, review what's there. Are there trees, shrubs, or overgrown plants to trim or prune? Are there old plantings to remove and replace with newer and healthier varieties? Can you use a red mulch to control garden weeds and create a natural contrast with the greenery?

Industry insiders say it's a good idea to use mature plants that are at least two to three feet high if you're planting shrubs or bushes. Anything smaller tends to look cheap, and anything much bigger will hide other improvements like fresh paint or newly dug flower gardens.

KEY INSIGHT

Some real estate investors appear to abandon the exterior upkeep of a rental property's landscape once the new plants are in place. That's a mistake. Protect your investment in landscaping by arranging to have a gardener or landscaper visit the property on a weekly or biweekly basis until the property sells or rents. Without regular attention while the property is vacant, the money you spend on landscaping may be wasted.

---

4. Replace Windows and Doors

New windows across the front of a home offer another quick fix with instant curb appeal. If the existing windows are outdated, consider replacing them. At approximately $30 a pair from a home improvement store, you also may want to think about adding new window shutters to dress up the front of the house.

Always (and that means *always*) replace the front door if it is outdated. At the very least, apply a fresh coat of paint to the front door and install new gold or silver hardware, a kick plate, and a new door knocker. That will set you back less than $100.

If the home you bought features a beautiful old front door, consider refurbishing it rather than replacing it.

5. Install a New Mailbox

The mail delivered to this property will be addressed to the people who live there. Making sure the mailbox matches the exterior color of their new home is another nice touch for improved curb appeal.

HOW MUCH SHOULD YOU SPEND?

How do you know how much to spend on curb appeal improvements? The basic rule is to ask yourself if you're adding value or cutting corners. If all the front door needs to look great is two coats of paint, go for it. If the painted door looks awesome but the doorknob is loose or the knocker is missing, those are corners you should not cut.

KEY INSIGHT

Your buyer or renter will be motivated at some level by emotion and you want to heighten the positive experience of touring this property. Will a new front door make a deal? Probably not. Could a bad front door break a deal? Yes. Be honest about the business impacts of your choices.

27

Run If You Spot Any of the Top Three Reno Red Flags

While there are a lot of single-family homes on the US distressed property market, some of these properties need a lot of work, while others are located in neighborhoods with few buyers and renters. You want to be buying a deeply discounted property that just needs some work, not a structural do-over. As you move through the renovation stage, you must keep your eyes open and make good decisions.

Insight 22 talks about why kitchen and bathroom renovations have to be on the reno "need" versus "want" side of the budget ledger but still be efficient, effective, and economical. Regardless of whether you want to renovate a home for the rental market or to flip it, you have to be able to rehab that home efficiently, effectively, and economically every time. If you can't, the deal is not for you. If you can't answer the three E's affirmatively, identify the problem and deal with it. A little proactive action up front will save you cash and reduce headaches down the road.

KEY INSIGHT

When you make yourself answer tough questions about what "has" to be done during a property renovation, you emphasize the "thinking" part of the process. Doing so reduces the chance that decisions will be made based on emotions. This approach helps you look ahead. When you know how you want a project to end, it's easier to put in place all of the steps you need to meet that goal.

MAKE SURE YOUR PROJECT IS EFFICIENT

This question is really about *how* you plan to proceed versus the specifics of *what* you plan to do. Answering this query honestly is critical to your success at renovating for the buy-and-hold or buy-and-flip markets. Since time is your most precious commodity, be conscious of how you spend your time on any renovation project. Novice investors sometimes "feel better" when they micromanage details, but this is most likely not a good use of your time or resources.

Always play your strengths and delegate your weaknesses. This allows your team members to focus on their skills while you work with yours. For example, once your budget and scope of work are determined, let your contractors do their jobs. This gives you time to focus on an exit strategy for the property, as well as shop for the next deal. It also frees you up to communicate with the contractors and stay on top of the project details that warrant your attention.

KEEP THE PROJECT FOCUSED ON WHAT'S EFFECTIVE

Here, the focus is on the final product or *what* you plan to do. Is the project going to produce the intended result? Can project timelines be met? Will your exit strategy timelines work? If you plan to rent the property, your decisions will be different than if you plan a retail flip. It's easy to spend more money—the trick is to ensure your spending supports your strategy.

As the old saying goes, make sure your ladder is leaning against the right house before you start your work.

KEY INSIGHT

When you renovate a home to sell it, the speed of that sale factors into the effectiveness of your business strategies, so include the cost of a professional cleaning in your original bid. The general contractor will most likely subcontract the job, but this is one of the best ways to make sure your rehabbed house isn't full of dust when it's time to put the house on the market. And while someone else is busy cleaning, you can be shopping for your next deal.

STICK TO ECONOMICAL OPTIONS

Renovation budgets are notoriously subjective. Your goal is to make renovation choices that make sense for your strategic plan. While you can skin the rehabbed cat a thousand ways, you must focus on your buyer or renter and make sure your project sticks to a realistic price point. Figure out how much money it will take to fill or sell this property at that price point, and then make renovation decisions that fit the budget.

KEY INSIGHT

The goal on every project, whether rental or resale, is to take one of the worst homes on the block and make it one of the best. That enables you to target homes at deep discounts. But that strategy only works if you can make the home something your target customer wants to rent or buy. This is why it's necessary to get several bids for each reno project—you never want to be stuck with just one choice! It's also why you should pay such close attention to your renovation budget. You know what needs to be done, and you don't want to leave out essential items that will "save" you money.

THE TOP THREE RENO RED FLAGS

Sticking to the three E's will help you avoid making expensive mistakes on a property renovation, but knowing what to do is only part of the equation. It's also helpful to zero in on what *not* to do.

The three biggest mistakes investors make involve the following:

- Buying the wrong house (as in paying too much or buying a property qualified tenants and buyers will shun because of location).

- Not planning for change orders, renovation surprises, or budgeting for contingencies.

- Giving your general contractor more than 25 percent as an initial payment to start work.

The good news about these three mistakes is that each one generally comes onto the renovation scene waving a giant red flag. Investors who tell you they didn't see these problems coming simply weren't paying attention to the warning signs. The real estate market is booming with investment opportunities, but when opportunity knocks, the smart investor takes responsibility for what's going to happen when he opens the door. Due diligence is about making sure a deal works long before you are financially responsible for a property.

As part of that due diligence, be on the lookout for the following three red flags.

Red Flag 1: Deeply Discounted Sales Price

Let's be realistic. You are taking an educated risk on every property renovation and you should be prepared for at least some surprises even on a cosmetic rehab. But finding out you need to upgrade light fixtures for a couple of hundred dollars is very different from discovering you have structural issues with a house's foundation. The latter could entail hiring structural engineers or architects and having to jack up and re-pour pilings or beams, actions that could break every window in the house and cause more structural issues with the roof.

The point here is that you need to find out what's behind a deeply discounted sales price, because this is one red flag you never want to discover waving over a property *after* you've already bought it. Not every home on the market is an investment deal and there is absolutely no reason to invest in a project with major structural issues. These "deals" may be significantly discounted, but your profit margins will be consumed by the structural remedy that is required, and few investors are able to make a deal like this work.

Buying the wrong house to renovate can also be a matter of location. See Insight 12 about recognizing a bad neighborhood.

PROCEED WITH ENTHUSIASM!

Make Your Money on the Low-Hanging Fruit

Smart real estate investors are attracted to discounted housing prices, but they stick to the low-hanging fruit. They will paint, they will update carpet, kitchens, and baths and they will revamp the landscape to improve curb appeal, but they will steer clear of houses with structural or foundation issues because too many things can go wrong.

If you have multiple renovation projects, it helps to take a cookie-cutter approach to your rehab. That way your general contractors know exactly what you want and there are few surprises on their end either. And that familiarity will have a positive impact on bids; contractors who know they can deliver what you expect want to earn your business because they too can make money with fewer hassles.

That doesn't mean that you should never consider deals that can entail rather pricey property upgrades. But you can manage projects that need major work, because you will know in advance what the work will cost based on the reliable information you receive from your contractors.

The moral of this story is all about good business. Hit singles and doubles again and again and you won't have to worry about the grand slam. It's less stressful—and you'll still win the game!

Red Flag 2: No Time for Proper Planning

Never let a "lack of time" interfere with your due diligence. You need to accept the fact that there will be change orders or surprises on every deal you do, because no project will ever come in at the exact penny your budget predicted. You can have projects that will come in under budget—and those are a nice surprise—but realistically, it's more likely you will go slightly over your budget. That's only a problem if you don't plan for that possibility, or you paid too much for the property to begin with. The latter is the tougher situation, because you're stuck with the deal, and will need to find creative ways to make it work (or cost you less).

This is one red flag that investors should be waving for themselves, especially if you're swimming in the foreclosed properties pool! In this market niche, your deals must be based on the best information you can find. Rush that process and you'll pay.

On the plus side, once you accept that change orders are a fact of life, you can deal with them relatively easily by building a 20-percent contingency into your budget. This 20-percent contingency is probably even more important for investors buying single-family homes that are in foreclosure. Foreclosed homes usually have not been taken care of properly by the previous owner or tenant. Some of the things you may need to fix may not be identifiable up front, especially if you buy a property "as is" without conditions or a formal inspection.

Your team is very important when it comes to planning. Surround yourself with trustworthy professionals who know what to look for. Are the market fundamentals in place to make this property work? Do you have reliable cost estimates to plug into your budget? (If it turns out you don't need to replace a roof or HVAC system, great! But you'll want to be prepared for what you find when you assume ownership.)

As always, the more due diligence, the better, especially if you are a foreigner or newbie investor.

KEY INSIGHT

A 20-percent budget contingency is a standard used in the construction industry. On a $10,000 budget, that means adding a cushion of $2,000. If it turns out that money is not needed, it goes right to profit. Not bad!

As noted in Insight 24 about the big four renos, always plan budget for doing the big four unless you know with certainty that something's not needed. (For example, you may know the deal has a two-year-old roof because you've bought the same type of product in the same type of neighborhood, so you won't have to budget for work to the roof.) Also, keep your budget numbers real by working with contractors you trust. Even with the 20-percent contingency, you may still go over budget, but if the deal is good you should still come out of it with a decent profit. Remember, it's all about the singles and doubles, not the grand slams.

Red Flag 3: Your Contractor Wants More Than 25 Percent Down

This red flag is easy to spot and easy to deal with. Never—ever—pay a contractor more than 25 percent of the total budget to start a project. If the contractor needs more than that to work with you, find a new contractor. Make no exceptions to this rule. Contractors will give you every excuse in the book for why they need more money to start, but don't listen. If they need more than 25 percent, they are either using your funds to cover overhead from their last project that didn't go as well as planned, or they don't have the appropriate lines of credit or cash reserves to run their company. Either way, if you see this red flag, search for a new contractor.

Canadian investors who ignore this red flag risk a hefty financial lesson, and in the worst-case scenario, the 25-percent deposit you give a contractor to start a property renovation could disappear into thin air before any work is done. A 20-percent contingency will cover some of your loss and you may still be able to get your rehab finished and make a profit. Without that contingency, though, you've got nothing.

KEY INSIGHT

Use common sense when scheduling and releasing payments to your general contractor. A practical suggestion is giving 25-percent draws equal to the scope of work that is completed to your satisfaction. Release each draw only after a thorough walk-through. The final draw is always the most important payment you make to a contractor. Unless you are 110-percent satisfied with the finished product, do not release the final payment. You want to make sure the contractor has an economic incentive to complete the project to the agreed specifications.

28

Hire the Right Property Manager

Canadian real estate investors who want to buy and hold rental property in the United States must make quality property management a top priority. Next to picking the right property, this is the most important decision you will make. This management must be effective, efficient, and economical, and it must be in place at all times. If you believe that money follows management, then you will see this as an area that demands constant investor vigilance, because property management can make or break your buy-and-hold investment.

You will want to make sure any property manager you hire has a good track record, has other houses or properties under administration, is reliable, has a high degree of personal integrity, and has the ability to manage your asset. Do a thorough background check, and ask for references of satisfied clients that your property manager has worked with.

It's also good to do a check with the HOA (Home Owners Association) because the manager's financial health will help or hinder the way your asset is managed. So we highly encourage you to do your due diligence to get the right property manager, because that will be the person safeguarding your wealth and your financial future.

To help Canadian investors increase the odds of finding the right property manager for their US properties, here are seven golden questions that experienced investors ask when they're hiring property managers for distressed properties they've purchased and renovated for the buy-and-hold rental market.

KEY INSIGHT

When you're investigating contractors, you should get quotes from three people or companies. When you're looking to hire a property manager, you need to double that and interview at least six potential property managers. Always let prospective hires know you are interviewing five others and that this additional attention to quality comes from your commitment to getting the right people for the job. Your goal is to build a long-term relationship with a property manager who sees the benefits of that quality-first approach.

ZERO IN ON EXCELLENCE: SEVEN QUESTIONS TO ASK POTENTIAL PROPERTY MANAGERS

1. Does the property management company already manage property in the area where my property is located, and does it manage the type of home I own?

   If the management company already has rentals under management in your specific area, meaning the same neighborhood or relatively close by, it is much more likely to be able to meet your needs. If their other properties are farther away, move on. Proximity to the properties they manage is critical.

   Also make sure the company manages the type of home that is in your portfolio. If your homes are 1,200 square feet in a working class "regular Joe" neighborhood, you don't need a property manager who typically works with tenants of higher-end homes. Ditto for the property manager whose experience is with multi-family properties.

2. Do you own your own investment property?

   Always ask about the property manager's personal real estate investing experience. Property managers who have "skin in the game" have better knowledge about what the role entails, almost always do a better job, and it always shows in the company's performance. You want your property manager to have a "landlord mentality." That can be learned, but it's easier to perfect if the manager owns rental property.

3. How many houses does the company have under management?

   Volume is also an asset. If a property management company manages less than 100 properties in a market with a population of more than one million people, market-savvy US investors would consider them a very under-developed management company. You want experience.

Also find out how many different owners the company manages for. If they have 200 units under management, but 198 of them are with one owner, be wary. If that owner pulls his portfolio, the property management company could go out of business that day. For stability, you want a property management company whose portfolio includes various owners.

KEY INSIGHT

If you want to grow your real estate portfolio in a particular part of a city, aim to be your property management company's biggest client. You may be rewarded with discounts for your high volume.

---

4. What are the management company's rent collection and eviction policies and procedures?

    If a prospective property manager can't give you a direct response, move on. This is an essential part of property management and you need someone who knows how to do this—and do it well.

    A good management company will have a very clear system and a no-nonsense strategy for rent collection and evictions. This is a fundamental business priority: your mortgage payment is due every month, no matter what. Poorly conceived and/or implemented rent collection and eviction processes put your investment at risk.

KEY INSIGHT

It's not uncommon for rental collection and eviction issues to wreak major financial havoc in the early days of real estate investing. Don't let poor management of your US properties make your business a statistic! Charity is a great thing, but it's not a good fit with a rental portfolio. Keep the two completely separate by making sure your heart never gets bigger than your head.

---

5. What is the property management company's vacancy ratio? What are the days-on-the-market stats for the current portfolio? How do these compare

to the overall single-family market for that area? What will the company do to make sure my property is rented?

Vacancy rates and days-on-the-market are as important as rent collection and eviction policies and procedures. Make sure they are a priority for the management company you hire.

This can be especially critical for Canadian investors as it's easy to lose sight of your basic cash-flow priorities when you're facing a spectacular deal. Remember that it doesn't matter how great your deal is. If you can't keep that discount-priced home filled and performing, that great deal can put your entire investment portfolio at risk.

Drill potential property managers about their strategies to get and keep tenants:

- What type of marketing do you use to fill vacancies?
- Why is your approach successful?
- What type of signage, websites, ads, etc. do you currently use?
- Can you show me what you're doing for other owners?
- Do you have any ideas about how my properties should be marketed to give them an edge?
- Do you charge extra fees for marketing? (If they do, that's bad! This should be included.)

6. What are the company's fees?

This question is very important. How do these people earn their money? A good management company usually gets a one-time fee for filling the property (a placement fee) and then a percentage of collected rents. If the company is not collecting rents, they shouldn't be getting paid!

Fees vary across the country and within states—a standard rate would be 10 to 12 percent, but fees can be as low as 8 percent and as high as 14 percent. Do your research and make sure you know what is reasonable before you start interviewing property managers. Be mindful of what's behind different rates. In property management, as with most service industries, you get what you pay for.

If you have no plans to buy multiple properties in the United States, you may consider offering a management company a higher rate to ensure they manage your smaller portfolio. A little extra will reduce your income and make sure you can sleep at night in Canada.

Avoid a management company that uses maintenance or repairs as a profit center. You want a company that takes care of this part of the job at par pricing without add-on fees. You also should establish a procedure for repairs over a certain dollar amount. Some investors don't let a management company undertake a repair over $250 without their permission.

7. How will I get my money and statements?

This is another area over which you should have full control. A good management company should have auto-deposit available for you into whatever bank account you choose to receive your rental profits. The company should have a specific date for depositing the rental profits and you should also receive a management statement every month. That statement will review the performance of the property by showing rents collected, expenses and fees, and the balance to be dispersed to the owner.

Make sure the statements you're getting are simple. If you can't understand the statements, then you can't manage your investments. For efficiency, ask for soft copies (email) of these reports, and reconcile every statement and have a staff bookkeeper or accountant do the same. The extra set of eyes is an important way to ensure accuracy.

KEY INSIGHT

When a real estate investor takes the time to do a thorough job of finding the right property manager, he or she satisfies a primary requirement of any solid due diligence strategy: always do your homework. The key to a buy-and-hold investment is the quality of ongoing management, so take your time, choose wisely and never be afraid to fire your property manager and redo the whole process if your expectations are not met.

---

29 Make Money by Delegating to Your Property Manager

Experienced real estate investors often say they make their money when they buy a property. That's true. Investors in the US distressed real estate market know that they can make more money on houses they buy at significantly discounted prices. The painfully simple secret to understanding the numbers side of this business is encapsulated in an age-old slogan: buy low and sell high. While that's tough to do in the stock market, real estate investing is a different story. You may not ever sell at the absolute peak of a market or buy at the market's lowest point, but as long as you stick to investment fundamentals and invest in properties with positive cash flow, your business will profit.

KEY INSIGHT

Make cash flow an investment fundamental. As long as a property is in a cash-flow position, you've got time to tweak your exit strategy.

But there is more to real estate investment success than the wisdom of positive cash flow and a buy-low-sell-high strategy. If you're going to make money in this market niche, you also have to understand that this is a numbers game where your relationships with people will help you score the points you need to tally a profit. From this perspective, management is about more than sound business strategies, it's about building relationships with the folks who can help you put those strategies in place.

PUT YOUR MONEY TO WORK

Insight 28 walks you through the seven best questions to ask prospective property managers. Here, we want to emphasize why property management is so important, especially on buy-and-hold rentals.

Finding a good property manager takes work, and some readers may scratch their heads and ask why they need a property manager when it's going to cost 8 to 14 percent of their rental fees. As a Canadian investing in the US property market, you must be honest about what you can and cannot do in terms of managing a property from hundreds or thousands of kilometers away. This is one area where an investor can micromanage her investment all the way to the red-ink side of the business ledger.

As an investor, you do not need to do everything yourself. That one-man show is required if you're day-trading stocks. In real estate, the lesson is simple: the more you leverage other people's time and expertise, the more successful you will be. Letting someone else manage your properties gives you more time to find deals and to develop relationships with other people who will be good additions to your investment team.

One of the biggest mistakes investors make is thinking that property management is all about regular property checks and minor repairs, or hiring a qualified tradesperson when additional work is needed. If that's where your knowledge of property management is stuck, here are some things you need to think about.

A property manager has consistent access to your property because he lives in the area. A property manager is all of the following:

- In the right place at the right time to make sure your property maintains its value. If you've taken the worst house on the street and made it the best, you have a vested interest in making sure that property maintains its value. But if you spend all of your own time doing that, there's no time left for investing.

- The first person to know if rent is or isn't paid.

- Ideally situated to develop and put in place a proven system to deal with rent issues as soon as they arise. (No flying in to meet tenants, no long-distance excuses.)

- In the right place to keep you up-to-date on your investment's performance. A property manager submits regular statements that show rents collected, expenses and fees, and the balance dispersed to the owner.

- The right person for the right job. The manager has a good working knowledge of the market where your property is located. He knows where to find local tradespeople when needed and he can be trusted to get minor repairs done without bothering the investor—up to the limit you have established (recommended at $250). All of this market knowledge is essential to keeping your units rented and cash flowing.

With the right people in place, you will find that you will spend remarkably little time worrying about whether you "know enough" or are "smart enough" to invest in real estate. Property management is one of those areas where delegation is critical to an investor's success. These people can help you make money. It's that simple.

PROFESSIONAL PROPERTY MANAGEMENT PAYS FOR ITSELF

In sum, the real estate investment business is a good example of an enterprise where money follows management. It is imperative that you manage your systems and team, but you need to understand that growth and control enjoy an inverse relationship. If you micromanage in an area like property management, you compromise your ability to make money by buying property.

You need to manage people and strategies, but it's okay to let others do the hands-on work.

KEY INSIGHT

Success comes from an attitude that celebrates cooperation over competition. Don't try to compete with the people you meet in the real estate investment community. Instead, think of every person you meet as a potential expert at something that will enhance your life and business. Your goal should be to add reciprocal value to these relationships by helping others.

---

30 | Set the Rules Up Front with Your Property Manager

We've reviewed the important questions you need to ask to help you hire the right property manager for your US rental properties, and we've discussed why good property management will make you money. So do we really need to talk about the value of good communication with your property manager? Yes. And that's because this fundamental is one that far too many investors are willing to address with lip service instead of action.

If you plan to take your Canadian dollars and use them to buy distressed or any other properties in the United States, really consider how the distance between you and your property manager can affect your investment. Real estate investment is a great way to put your money to work for your long-term wealth. But that does not mean you get to park your money in an investment property and leave the country.

As with most relationships, the key to good communication boils down to making sure that all parties know and understand the rules. That means setting the rules up front, not as you go.

GET YOUR COMMUNICATIONS PLAN IN PLACE

This is one relationship where a real estate investor can expect to reap what she sows. As soon as you hire a property manager, set the foundation of your communications plan and be thorough and consistent. (If you've stuck to the ideas in Insight 28 about hiring the right property manager, this individual already knows how you work and what you expect.)

A full-time US investor with more than one hundred properties in his portfolio is in daily contact with his property management company. As these all are rental properties, and a portfolio of that size has a great number of moving parts. While daily contact may not be appropriate on a smaller portfolio, real estate investors must be clear about what they need to keep their investment on track.

Monthly Reports

Monthly reports are standard fare. Information about rents, expenses, and cash flow is essential to your portfolio's sustainability. Do not compromise on this point. Every investor needs a monthly report.

Personal Contact

Some investors will physically meet with their property managers once a week. While weekly face-to-face meetings are only necessary when you own a significant number of properties, you must take care to never let a property manager think your absence equates to disinterest. If face-to-face meetings are not pragmatic given distance and portfolio size, then monthly reports should be supported by regular phone conversations and communication updates over email and text messaging (see the upcoming section "Use Technology Wisely").

Weekly phone or face-to-face meetings may run thirty to sixty minutes. Use the time to address maintenance issues, collections, vacancies, move outs, evictions, and Keys for Cash program candidates (see Insight 31).

KEY INSIGHT

Money follows management. Regular communication with your property manager is the best way to keep abreast of management decisions and issues. No matter how good a manager is, the property's success hinges on your money. If the ball gets dropped, it's your money that is at risk, not the manager's.

STICK TO BUSINESS

Make sure your regular meetings are informative and efficient. Some investors have their property managers prepare a detailed report every week and then use that to guide their face-to-face or phone meetings. This boosts productivity by keeping the conversation on track. Meetings detract from the time you spend finding deals (or enjoying a life where your money's working even when you're not). Remember that your property manager probably feels the same way; these meetings must be productive because they cut into his hands-on management time.

USE TECHNOLOGY WISELY

Emails and texts can save you and your property manager a lot of time. If you have a good rapport with your property manager and trust his recommendations, you can develop a communications plan whereby you use email or texts to review and approve bids, authorize expenditures, or address other issues the manager cannot handle without your consent.

KEY INSIGHT

You can run your business, or let it run you. As a foreign investor living a long way from your investments, you must stay on top of property management decisions and be prepared to step in if a property manager needs direction. But the more you can delegate to your manager, the better. After all, that's what you pay the manager to do.

As you set your communications plan in motion, make sure your property manager knows you have four expectations that must be met.

1. Keep the Properties Full

A good property manager will fill your properties quickly with *qualified tenants*. These are tenants who can pay the rent! Make sure your property manager understands that you know what happens when a property manager slams unqualified tenants into your vacancies. Tell him this causes a high turnover rate and often leads to property damage. As such, it runs counter to a sustainable business strategy that will protect your investment and keep your property manager employed.

Let him know that you want your property to be product and price competitive with other homes on the market in your area. If he has issues with what constitutes product or price competitiveness, or his values change over time, the property manager needs to address those concerns with you.

2. Apply the Three E's to Maintenance and Repairs

Talk to your property manager about expenses. Tell him you want maintenance and repairs to be effective, efficient, and economical, and that you will need assurances that that is what he is delivering. (You may want to see some evidence of bids, for example.)

Quality renovations generally cut maintenance and repair costs, which keeps tenants and property managers happy. But properties sometimes do require maintenance and repair. Work with your property manager to satisfy reasonable tenant requests even when they aren't expected or they seem unwarranted. You do not have to meet every request, but you may want to address those that are reasonable. Again, you want your property manager to talk to you about situations like this. Together, you can use the three E's to keep a long-term tenant happy.

3. Manage the Day-to-Day Issues

Let your property manager know you want him to handle the day-to-day issues that arise. That's what a good property manager does. A good investor supports a good property manager. This approach lets you both do what you're good at.

4. Find Resolutions, Not Confrontations

Communication is a two-way street. If either you or your property manager does not feel like your respective expectations are being met, you need to point out why you are not satisfied and be prepared to resolve the issue quickly.

When resolution is not possible, skip the confrontation and hire a new property manager. This is a business decision, so keep emotions out of it and act swiftly. The longer you take to make the right decision, the sooner you'll pay for it. Procrastination is your enemy.

31

Be Smart about Rent Collection

We can't stress enough the importance of making sure you have quality property management in place with a solid plan for collecting the rent. This fundamental is critical regardless of whether your revenue properties are in Canada or the United States.

One of the best rental collection policies comes from a US investor who specializes in the distressed property market. He buys his properties at significant discounts, renovates them to make them market ready, and then works with his property managers to put in place what he calls the *Keys for Cash* program.

It is, bar none, the best passive approach to handling *non-performing* (delinquent) tenants you will ever come across. If you want to be smart about rent collection and save yourself a lot of headaches and cash, you need to adopt the Keys for Cash program.

WARNING

The Keys for Cash program might shock novice investors and those still thinking about real estate investing, because they may be prone to emotional responses to a business decision. If you read what follows and don't think the Keys for Cash program is necessary, take heed. You'll find that the Keys for Cash program is simple and effective and veterans of the industry love it because it protects their investments and integrity.

FROM DELINQUENT TO DELIVERED

If your tenant can't pay the rent, he is already in a financially stressful situation. Understand intellectually what that means. You can feel bad for him, but if you really want to help, make sure your choices do not compound the tenant's fiscal issues and exacerbate your own. Know that when you allow tenants to take advantage of your emotional response to their plight, you will pay the piper because you will make the problem more difficult and expensive to solve.

The Keys for Cash program works like this: Let's say the rent is due, in full, on the first of every month, with no exceptions. If a tenant is late, your property manager will send out a three-day pay-or-quit letter. It notifies the tenant that he has three days to pay the rent or quit the property. That letter should include an option for Keys for Cash to the delinquent tenant. This option stipulates the following:

> To avoid eviction, you, the tenant, have an option to move out of the house completely, including all of your belongings, within seven days of receiving this letter. The home is returned broom swept, cleaned, and in the same or better condition to when you moved in. In return, the owner will not pursue the eviction or you for the delinquent funds and will not report you to the credit bureaus for eviction, which will affect you finding another home to move to. In return, you, the tenant, will receive $XXX* cash in seven days after a satisfactory inspection is completed by the property manager, at which time you will turn over the keys to the property manager and receive your money.
>
> By signing this agreement, you, the tenant, agree to forfeit any security deposit and will not pursue the owner for any further losses or liabilities of any kind in the future pertaining to this lease.
>
> *Sum to range from $100 to $500, depending on the rent or situation.

This letter must be signed and dated by the tenant and you or your property manager. This shows that all of the terms of the Keys for Cash program were accepted and that you have the acceptance in writing, regardless of whether the tenant does or does not meet all the requirements.

KEY INSIGHT

If your property manager will not adopt the Keys for Cash program, find a new property manager. Rent collection is essential to your cash-flow business strategy. Do not let your deal be compromised by delinquent tenants.

What you're doing is very smart. The sooner you can get your non-performing asset back with as little damage as possible, the more money you make or avoid losing, period. The eviction process is a long and very expensive procedure. It includes eviction costs, loss of rents, and damages to the property left by an unhappy tenant. Why not allow the tenant to leave with some dignity and get your asset back in great shape so you can get it filled again as soon as possible?

IT'S ALL ABOUT THE BUSINESS

Some new investors balk at the idea that they should give a tenant's security deposit back when the tenant defaults on rent, but you can look at this differently. From a purely business perspective, this is money you would return to a renter if the lease was up or the renter was planning to move out and had not damaged the property.

You may also consider giving delinquent tenants a good recommendation to their next landlord if they were good tenants up to this point, after taking steps to make sure their situations are legitimate. (Perhaps they just need to downsize to a cheaper rental because of job loss, health issues, etc.) Out of respect to the next landlord, you should explain that the tenant was delinquent, but also tell the landlord that the tenant agreed to the provisions of the Keys for Cash program and met all its requirements. This is about doing business in good faith. However, do not be naïve about the situation, either. Your property manager should meet the delinquent tenant at the property with a locksmith on the move-out date. As soon as the property inspection is complete, the locksmith should change the locks. This is one more way to make sure the tenant understands that this is a business decision and you take your business seriously.

KEY INSIGHT

If you are going into the buy-and-hold rental real estate market, you need to accept and respect that tenants who pay, consistently and on time, are essential to whether your business succeeds or fails. Their rental payments are your income and without it, your business doesn't work.

Paying the rent on time is non-negotiable, but you can be flexible and exercise integrity to keep your assets performing. The Keys for Cash program is a great example of thinking outside the box and putting a solution to work.

PART IV

CROSS-BORDER TAX PLANNING

32

Understanding US Tax Laws

Experienced Canadian real estate investors know that their businesses must comply with Canadian tax law. They also know that quality tax and accounting advice can save them money, not because they are "avoiding" tax, but because tax and accounting professionals can help investors make sure they are not paying any more tax than they are legally required to pay.

Guess what? It works pretty much the same way for Canadian investors doing business in the US real estate market. You will be required to pay tax on the money you earn in the United States, but with good advice, you should never pay more than you are legally required to pay.

FILING A US TAX RETURN

A basic principle to remember is that anytime you earn income in the United States, you must file a US tax return as well as your Canadian return. Your property manager is usually responsible for tracking and filling out the income you receive and expenses you make on your investment property, and may help you prepare the paperwork. A knowledgeable property manager may even go so far as to fill out your US tax return for you.

One important consideration is the tax rates you will be paying. Any US federal or state tax you pay will be credited against the Canadian tax payable on the income. As an example, if you were to earn $8,500 per year from a US rental property you'll pay Uncle Sam about 10 percent. What are the implications for your Canadian tax? Let's imagine your total tax rate this year is an even 20 percent. The 10 percent you paid in the US would be credited against the 20 percent you owe to the Canada Revenue Agency, which means you only owe an additional 10 percent here in Canada. US tax rates are consistently lower than Canadian tax rates.

KEY INSIGHT

Real estate investors often talk about building an *investment team*. These are the people, like real estate agents, general contractors, home inspectors, lawyers, and accountants, who help you operate your investment property. It's essential to recognize that investing in US real estate is a significant shift from your domestic work. Make sure that your tax and legal professionals are familiar with US tax law.

GENERAL GUIDELINES

There are three key concepts that guide tax planning in the United States:

- Deductions
- Shifting tax brackets
- Entity structure

Deductions

As in Canada, the United States only taxes net income or income reduced by certain deductions, so the first way to reduce your taxes on your US investment income is to ensure that you take advantage of all allowable deductions.

There are two primary requirements for making an expense deductible. First, the expense cannot increase the value of the property and second, the expense has to be ordinary and necessary to the real estate business. An expense increases the value of the property when it causes the property to last longer or adds a feature to the property that will last more than a year. This is slightly different in Canada, where tax law stipulates a difference between an "upgrade" and "maintenance," with the latter being deductible. Upgrades generally have to be capitalized. For example, if you replace double-paned windows with triple-paned, the cost of the double-paned window you are replacing can be deducted from the total expense, and only the difference is capitalized.

Suppose you plan to rent out a single-family home you purchase in the United States through foreclosure. If the house needs serious work to get it into a condition so that someone will be willing to rent it, you hire contractors to go in and complete the upgrades. Some of the work they do will extend the life of the property—things like a new roof or an HVAC (heating and air conditioning) unit. These expenses are going to make the property last longer. The contractor also may do some renovations, such as adding a bedroom or converting a carport to a garage. These renovations add long-term value to the property.

Expenses that cause the property to last longer or that add a feature which increases the value of the property cannot be deducted immediately. Instead, they are added to the cost of the property and are depreciated over several years.

Expenses to pay contractors to complete maintenance, cleaning, or minor repairs to the property are treated differently. While they are certainly important in terms of making the property attractive to lease, they don't extend its life nor do they add long-term value. Because they simply make the house livable and provide curb appeal, these expenses don't have to be added to the cost of the property and depreciated. Instead, they can be deducted from any other US income. Similarly, utilities, property taxes, advertising, and insurance can also be deducted.

The key is to ensure that any expenses you deduct are ordinary and necessary for the real estate business. An ordinary expense is one that is common in the industry. Cleaning, yard care, taxes, and insurance all qualify. Other expenses may not qualify, with the most challenging of those related to travel, meals, and entertainment. In the meantime, just understand that expenses must be considered "necessary" to qualify for deduction. This means that the purpose of the expenses is to increase the income from the property. As long as you are spending the money with the intention of increasing your income or preventing a loss of income, then the expenses are necessary.

Deducting Mortgage Interest

Americans can write off the interest on their mortgages, as well as their property taxes, against any income they earn from an investment property, but Canadians cannot. However, if a Canadian has a US mortgage on his investment property or borrows in the United States to earn income there, the interest paid is deductible against his US income. If the Canadian borrows in Canada to buy US property or to make an investment there, the Canadian interest is not deductible in the United States, but is deductible against the income earned in the United States for Canadian tax purposes.

Shifting Tax Brackets

Like Canada, the United States uses a progressive income tax bracket system, which means the last dollar you earn is taxed higher than the first dollar you earn. The income tax brackets are different for single individuals versus married couples and for corporations versus individuals. If you are a single individual, your tax brackets in the United States would look like this for 2012:

- **10 percent** on taxable income from $0 to $8,700, plus
- **15 percent** on taxable income over $8,700 to $35,350, plus
- **25 percent** on taxable income over $35,350 to $85,650, plus
- **28 percent** on taxable income over $85,650 to $178,650, plus
- **33 percent** on taxable income over $178,650 to $388,350, plus
- **35 percent** on taxable income over $388,350

This means that the first $8,700 you earn is taxed at only 10 percent. If you earn $388,350, then everything over that is taxed at 35 percent. Obviously, one of the keys to reducing taxes in the United States is to use as many tax brackets as possible by splitting income across different adult family members, so that each person pays tax at a lower rate than one person would pay on the total income.

Corporations

In the United States, there are three types of corporations: S corporations, C corporations, and limited liability corporations. Only full-time residents of the United States can own S corporations, so we won't discuss them in this book. *C corporations* are the equivalent of Canadian corporations, and with tax rates up to 35 percent, pay some of the highest corporate rates in the industrialized world. For this reason, it is not ideal for Canadians investing in the United States to use an American corporation to invest in real estate. Have a look at the corporate tax rates for 2012:

Corporate Tax Rates

$0 to $50,000	15%
$50,000 to $75,000	$7,500 + 25% of excess over $50,000
$75,000 to $100,000	$13,750 + 34% of excess over $75,000
$100,000 to $335,000	$22,250 + 39% of excess over $100,000
$335,000 to $10,000,000	$113,900 + 34% of excess over $335,000
$10,000,000 to $15,000,000	$3,400,000 + 35% of excess over $10,000,000
$15,000,000 to $18,333,333	$5,150,000 + 38% of excess over $15,000,000
Over $18,333,333	Flat 35%

Investors might want to consider using a C corporation for two primary reasons: protecting themselves from personal liability for any accidents or incidents involving the property and taking advantage of the benefits of the 1031 exchange rules. The *tax-free 1031 exchange* (or the like-kind exchange) allows you to replace investment properties with similar properties within six months of the sale without paying tax on the proceeds. The drawbacks of using a C corporation are the high tax rates, as we noted, and the fact that you lose the right to be taxed on the proceeds at the lower capital gains rate that is available to individuals.

Entity Structure

Perhaps the most important way for Canadians to reduce the tax on their US real estate investments is to use the right structure to make the investment. Again, there are strong parallels to the Canadian system and the way a business structure affects tax planning. In both countries, an "entity" is merely a way to own and manage your real estate. A limited partnership is an entity, as are corporations and trusts. The United States also has limited liability companies and limited liability limited partnerships.

KEY INSIGHT

The right entity structure is essential if you want to avoid double taxation. It can even get you a Canadian tax credit. Pay attention!

The most important aspect of your entity structure is that you don't pay tax both in the United States and in Canada. In fact, if you set up your entity structure the right way, you will get a credit that you can take on your Canadian tax return for taxes paid in the United States. If you fail to structure your entity properly, you can easily pay tax twice—once in the United States and again in Canada.

The other critical reason to be careful with your US entity structure will become more apparent as you work through Part 5 of this book. It will highlight the fact that every tenant is a potential plaintiff, as is anyone else who visits your property, including contractors, property managers and, believe it or not, trespassers! Indeed, the fact that more than 95 percent of the lawsuits filed worldwide are filed in the United States is an issue for anyone who does business there. You will want to make sure that you are protected from potential lawsuits—and tax planning is an essential part of that asset protection plan.

33

Taking Title to Your US Property Investments

If you ask a US investor about the best way to structure your US real estate investments, that's what you'll get: advice that applies to US investors. Canadians investing in the US market should ensure that they choose a business structure that balances a few things: personal liability issues, avoiding double taxation where possible, and limiting income, capital gains, and estate taxes as far as legally possible. It may be that for any given investor, one or two of those interests will outweigh the others, but it is important to understand all your options clearly.

LIMITED LIABILITY CORPORATIONS

As an investor in the United States, you will no doubt hear about the limited liability corporation (LLCs) as an investment entity because this is structure that is most widely used by Americans investing in real estate. For Americans, the limited liability corporation gives them limited liability, and they can elect to be taxed on a personal basis.

Canadians, however, should be aware that the Canada Revenue Agency does not recognize LLCs, and as a result, any income tax paid in the United States is not credited against your Canadian income earned in the United States, resulting in double taxation.

CORPORATIONS

Another common investment vehicle for Americans is the C corporation, which we first mentioned in Insight 32. For Canadians, however, they are not a viable option due to high US corporate tax rates, and the fact that corporations cannot take advantage of the preferential treatment for capital gains as noted above.

In addition, Canadian corporations as investment vehicles should be avoided for these two types of properties:

- Investment properties, because you will have to pay high US corporate taxes plus a 5-percent branch tax.

- Personal property, because ownership of the property will be an imputed benefit to you and personal tax will be payable as a consequence. See Insight 35 for more.

WHAT OPTIONS DO CANADIAN INVESTORS HAVE?

We've talked about what entities don't work for Canadian investors. So what options do you have? The alternatives open to Canadians are to hold US property in the following ways:

- Personally
- Via a Canadian limited partnership
- Via a US limited partnership
- Via a US general partnership
- Via a two-tiered limited partnership
- Via trusts

Holding Property Personally

The benefit of holding property in your own name personally is that you do not have to pay the legal costs associated with setting up a corporation or a limited partnership structure—you are just buying a house. If this is your second home, and you are not earning any rental income on it, there will be no tax implications until you sell the property, when you may have a capital gain.

If the property is an investment, you will pay tax on any rental income you earn in the United States at personal rates, which are lower than Canadian tax rates; you will get credit for US taxes paid on this rental income on your Canadian return. If the property is held for more than one year, US capital gains tax in the amount of 15 percent will be payable on the resale for which you will receive a credit against any Canadian capital gains tax due on the sale.

Any US taxes paid are credited against the Canadian income tax you will pay on the income, so you avoid double taxation. Remember that, as Canadians, you are likely paying higher tax rates than the US tax payable—so the actual American rate you pay probably does not really matter in calculating your overall financial position.

Most states charge an additional state income tax—Arizona, for example, has a sliding scale from 2.59 to 4.54 percent. Canadian investors will be happy to hear that Texas, Nevada, and Florida are among the nine states that do not charge state income tax.

The disadvantages of holding property personally are that withholding tax may be required on any rental income you earn, as well as the proceeds of a sale of the property, and US estate tax may be payable on your death. In addition, in the event that there is an accident or other lawsuit involving the property, you could be personally liable for any damages.

Limited Partnerships

A limited partnership structure has the advantage of limiting your liability in the event you are sued for some incident or transaction relating to the property.

With a Canadian limited partnership, the limited partners are taxed at their personal rates for any rental income earned; the partnership must file an information return in the United States and in Canada. Because it is owned personally, if the property is held for more than one year, the personal capital gains rate of 15 percent applies, as opposed to owning via a corporation where you pay corporate tax rates. For a Canadian limited partnership, the rules relating to withholding tax apply. If you choose to use a US limited liability partnership, again your liability will be limited, with the advantage that there are no withholding requirements. Estate tax may be payable on your death (see below).

Another advantage of a US limited partnership is that it may be easier to secure financing from a US lender, particularly smaller banks.

US General Partnership

A US general partnership should comprise a Canadian limited partnership with a C corporation as the American partner. The advantage of this structure is that there is no withholding tax payable and it is easier to obtain financing in the United States. US estate tax may be payable on your death.

Two-Tiered Limited Partnership

This is an American limited partnership, which has as one of its members a Canadian limited partnership. It is essential that you secure legal services to set this up for you, because it is complicated. This structure has the advantage of allowing you to avoid estate tax. It also has the benefit of you being permitted to declare income personally. The sale of the property will attract a preferential capital gains tax rate.

As with the US limited partnership, this structure may make it easier to obtain financing from American lenders.

Trust

A *trust* is where property is held by one party for the benefit of another, so you can pass property to your beneficiaries while you are still alive. On your death, the property passes to the beneficiaries in accordance with the terms of the trust. This way, you avoid probate for this part of your estate. However, you should be aware that under US law, if the person who is the "real owner" of the property actually uses the property, it could be deemed to be part of that person's estate for tax purposes.

US ESTATE TAX

In Canada, there is no estate tax, but there is a deemed disposition on death, which can result in capital gains tax being payable. Capital gains tax, however, is not as punitive as estate tax.

US estate tax is calculated on worldwide assets as a proportion of the overall value of your estate. For 2012, the exemption threshold is set at $5 million, though this may be reduced to $1 million in the near future (a level it has been at in the past). Once the net value of your estate passes the threshold, US estate tax becomes payable. For the purposes of calculating the net value of your estate, the proceeds of your life insurance policies are included, which in Canada are tax free.

Thus, if your total net worth is $900,000, and you have investment properties in the United States worth $500,000, no estate tax is payable. If your net worth is $10 million, and you have investment properties in the United States worth $2 million, estate tax is payable on the $2 million, on a sliding scale based on the value of the estate, starting at 18 percent to a maximum rate of 35 percent. (These are 2012 rates. There is some commentary that the maximum rate will increase to 55 percent in 2013.) You should ask your tax advisor to assist you in calculating possible estate tax, because you have include a pro-rated unified tax credit that depends on when you purchased the property.

Because of the uncertainty about rates and the exemption threshold, it is best to use conservative figures in your tax planning.

For Canadians investors, a Canadian limited partnership may allow you to avoid US estate tax, by converting the limited partnership into a corporation for tax purposes on your US income tax return. This method has been accepted by the IRS to date; however, tax practices change and you should consult your tax advisor about your personal situation.

GIFT TAX

If a Canadian owns an asset in the United States and wishes to gift it, the applicable gift tax laws will apply. You will pay federal gift tax on any gift worth more than $13,000.

34   Deal with Depreciation

Depreciation is an accounting term that applies to the way you can spread the cost of an asset over a period of several years, in effect accounting for how the asset depreciates or drops in value over its lifespan. In real estate, deprecation enables investors to recover capital costs on items that depreciate over time. A relatively new fence on a property you just purchased may be worth $1,000 today, but it certainly won't be worth $1,000 when you sell the property five years from now. If you handle this issue properly, you can use the depreciated value of the fence to reduce your taxes every year you own that property.

Real estate investors can put depreciation to work for their businesses on both sides of the Canada–US border, but some tax advisors may question the wisdom of speeding up your depreciation timetable, because taking the depreciation now means a tax bill later (when you post a gain on the property at disposal).

Tax advisors familiar with the real estate investment market would disagree. They say you should take your tax savings up front and use them to invest in more assets that produce more depreciation. With this strategy in play, your tax liability vanishes—and you increase your earning power.

DEPRECIATION RECAPTURE

While US taxpayers can use depreciation to offset their ordinary income and real estate investors can use depreciation to cut their tax bills and free up more money for investment, they do that knowing that the offset will be *recaptured* by the IRS. That is to say, when the taxpayer sells the asset that was used to offset the ordinary income through depreciation, he will be taxed on the gain as if it were ordinary income, not capital gains.

When depreciation recapture is triggered after you sell a property that has been depreciated, two different calculations are used. The first is for real property and the second is for all other depreciated property, meaning everything from fences and light fixtures to drapery. Both calculations are based on you having a gain when you sell the property—if you do not have a gain, then you will not have depreciation recapture.

Let's say investor Tom sells his business computer for $500. Tom bought the computer for $1,500 and has taken $1,200 in depreciation. The computer's adjusted basis is $300 ($1,500 cost − $1,200 depreciation) and the gain on the sale is $200 ($500 sales price − $300 adjusted basis). Because there is a gain, depreciation recapture is triggered.

For personal property, depreciation recapture is the lesser of the total depreciation taken or the actual gain. In this example, the gain of $200 is less than the $1,200 taken in depreciation, so the depreciation recapture is $200. That depreciation recapture is triggered at Tom's ordinary tax rates.

If Tom sold his computer for $200, there would have been a loss of $100 ($200 sales price − $300 adjusted basis). With a loss, depreciation recapture is not triggered, because there's nothing to recapture.

KEY INSIGHT

Tax regulations are highly interconnected and one action typically triggers another. When a taxpayer takes a loss on the sale of an asset, for example, there is no depreciation recapture, but the taxpayer may qualify for ordinary loss treatment under other tax rules.

Recapture on Real Estate Property

If Tom sells a building for $200,000 and land improvements for $20,000, the situation is different. Here, the straight-line method of depreciation is required, which exempts the transaction from depreciation recapture. The *straight-line method* computes depreciation (or amortization) by dividing the difference between an asset's cost and its expected salvage value by the number of years it is expected to be used. This is the simplest way to calculate depreciation, as it spreads out the cost of an asset equally over its lifetime.

Assume the land improvements were depreciated over 15 years. This would be an accelerated method of depreciation, so there will be depreciation recapture if there is a gain on the land improvements. Depreciation recapture on real property is calculated on the amount of depreciation taken over what would have been allowed using the straight-line method of depreciation.

Let's say Tom took $12,000 of depreciation on the land improvements. The gain on the sale of the land improvements is $8,000 ($20,000 cost − $12,000 depreciation). Under the straight-line method, only $7,000 of the depreciation would have been allowed. The depreciation recapture is $5,000 ($12,000 depreciation taken − $7,000 depreciation using the straight-line method). The depreciation recapture will be taxed at a maximum rate of 25 percent.

In sum, the depreciation deduction provides a legal way to fast-track depreciation prior to disposal and can reduce your taxes, even if you don't spend any actual cash. The IRS will seek to recapture that depreciation when you dispose of the property, but you can turn that to your advantage too. When you deduct the depreciation of your real property, you are deducting it at your ordinary tax rate, with the highest rate being 35 percent. Since depreciation recapture is taxed at a maximum rate of 25 percent, you will reap a permanent tax savings of up to 10 percent on your US tax return. This will be a credit against the Canadian tax owing on the transaction.

KEY INSIGHT

It is a myth that taxes are out of our control. Taxpayers have a great deal of control over how much tax they pay. Tax avoidance or mitigation is the legal utilization of tax laws to your advantage. It has nothing to do with tax evasion, which is illegal.

35

Limit Your US Taxation if You're a Canadian Snowbird

Now that you've been introduced to some of the US tax rules that are important to real estate investors, let's look at how the rules apply and some of the potential tax pitfalls that await Canadians who "visit" the United States for several months of the year, especially if they sometimes rent out their homes-away-from-home. Since these properties are typically held personally, the tax issues differ from those held as investment properties. Selling that personal property may trigger nasty US tax implications that you may be able to avoid by planning ahead.

In this Insight we tell you about a few of the main tax issues Canadian snowbirds need to know.

RESIDENCE RULES

Canadian snowbirds who never spend more than 121 days in the United States in any tax year are not considered US residents for income tax purposes under the IRS's substantial presence test. If you spend more than that period of time in the United States, you are considered a US resident for income tax purposes, and you are required to file a US income tax return and report income from all sources, including income from Canada.

If a Canadian spends more than 183 days in the United States or spends less than 183 days but more than the formula amount, a US tax return must be filed. To calculate the *formula amount*, take the number of days in the United States this year, plus one third of the number of days last year, plus one sixth of the number of days the previous year. If the time spent is less than 183 days, but above the formula amount, then a Form 8840 can be filed to avoid filing a US tax return.

As an aside, it is also important that you are aware of the requirements of your provincial health-care plans. In Ontario, for example, if you are out of province for more than six months you can lose your health care. This is truly the worst situation: paying American income tax and losing your Canadian health care. The details of provincial health care vary from one province to the next, so ensure that you are complying with the relevant requirements.

RENTING OUT YOUR PROPERTY

Snowbirds who rent out their American condo or other real estate properties should be aware that a withholding tax of 30 percent normally applies to the gross amount of any rent paid to a resident of Canada on real estate located in the United States. Unlike withholding taxes on interest and dividends, this tax is not reduced by the Canada–US tax treaty.

Canadians can avoid the 30-percent gross withholding tax by filing a US tax return and electing to pay tax on net rental income. Then they will receive a refund for any taxes withheld, to the extent the withholding amount exceeds the tax payable. This is most likely to be advantageous where you are incurring significant expenses such as mortgage interest, maintenance, insurance, property management, and property taxes, since tax at the graduated rates will likely be substantially lower than the 30-percent withholding tax.

The election of the net rental income method applies for all future years and may be revoked only in limited circumstances. The election applies to all of an individual's rental real estate in the United States, but be aware that a state tax (and possibly a city tax) also may be payable on the rental income if the election is made on the federal return.

Once the election is made, the taxpayer should give IRS Form W-8ECI to the tenant, and the 30-percent tax withholding will not be required.

SELLING YOUR PROPERTY

If a Canadian sells real estate located in the United State, a withholding tax of 10 percent of the gross sales price is normally payable under the Foreign Investment in Real Property Tax Act (FIRPTA). The tax withheld can be offset against the US income tax payable on any gain realized on the sale and refunded if it exceeds the tax liability. The 10-percent withholding requirement on the gross sale price applies regardless of the seller's *adjusted basis* (the net cost of an asset after adjusting for tax-related items) in the property.

There are two exceptions to FIRPTA's 10-percent withholding requirement that may reduce or eliminate the requirement. Exception number one kicks in if the sale price is less than US$300,000 and the purchaser intends to use it as a residence. The buyer need not be a US resident.

For this exception to apply, the purchaser must have definite plans to live at the property for at least half of the time that the property is in use during each of the two years following the sale. The gain on the sale still will be taxable in the United States and, therefore, a US tax return must be filed.

Exception number two involves a *withholding certificate*. A Canadian obtaining a withholding certificate from the IRS on the basis that the expected US tax liability will be less than 10 percent of the sales price is allowed reduced or eliminated withholding. The certificate will indicate what amount of tax should be withheld by the purchaser, rather than the full 10 percent.

If an application for a withholding certificate with respect to a transfer of a US real property interest is submitted to the IRS, but has not been received by the IRS at the time of the transfer, the buyer must withhold 10 percent of the amount realized. However, the amount withheld, or a lesser amount as determined by the IRS, does not need to be reported and paid over to the IRS until the twentieth day following the IRS's final determination with respect to the application for a withholding certificate.

The buyer's legal representative generally will hold the 10-percent withholding in an escrow account until the withholding certificate is received. The seller will then be refunded the amount permitted pursuant to the withholding certificate. If the seller does not apply for the withholding certificate, the seller must wait until after year-end to file a tax return to claim a refund for the excess of the withholding amount over the ultimate tax liability.

GAIN: FILING REQUIREMENTS

For income tax purposes, a Canadian investor must file a US federal tax return and report the gain on the sale of US real estate. The resulting tax will be offset by the FIRPTA tax withheld. An individual also may be subject to state income tax withholding and filing requirements.

If an individual owned US property and has been resident in Canada since before September 27, 1980, he can likely take advantage of the Canada–US tax treaty to reduce the gain. In this case, only the gain accruing since January 1, 1985, will be taxed. This transitional rule does not apply to business properties that are part of a permanent establishment in the United States.

To claim the benefit under the treaty, a Canadian will need to make the claim on a US tax return and include a statement containing certain specific information about the transaction.

FOREIGN TAX CREDIT

US tax paid on the sale of US property will generate a foreign tax credit that may be used to reduce the Canadian tax on the sale; however, if the amount of the gain taxed in Canada is reduced because of the principal residence exemption, the foreign tax credit available may be limited. In addition, a strengthening Canadian dollar in relation to the US dollar may result in a larger taxable gain in the United States than in Canada. The opposite would be true if the Canadian dollar declines in value from the date of acquisition.

ESTATE TAXES

As noted earlier, US estate taxes can also impose a burden on the estates of Canadians who own US real estate when they die. Possible ways to minimize these taxes include holding the property through a Canadian corporation, splitting interest, obtaining non-recourse debt financing, and using a two-tiered partnership structure.

Holding Property Through a Canadian Corporation

If you hold business real estate through a Canadian corporation rather than personally, no US estate tax will apply. This is because the shares of the Canadian corporation are not considered "property" within the United States. Ordinarily, if US real estate is used personally by a Canadian share-holder, for Canadian tax purposes the Canadian would have to recognize a taxable benefit equal to the value of the rental usage of the property, unless the shareholder pays the rental value to the corporation.

The CRA used to have a liberal administrative policy of not assessing a taxable shareholder benefit for personal use of a corporate-owned US vacation property if it was owned by a "single-purpose corporation" that met certain requirements. The CRA recently revoked this policy for property acquired by or transferred to a single-purpose corporation after 2004. Prior to that ruling, a single-purpose corporation's sole objective was to hold property for the personal use or enjoyment of the shareholder. Because the corporate ownership provided an estate tax shelter, it was a good tax-planning tool for Canadians owning personal-use property in the United States.

Today, single-purpose corporations that are properly structured to acquire US real estate prior to 2005 continue to be covered by the CRA's initial policy. For US estate tax purposes, there may be an issue as to whether the IRS will respect the single-purpose corporation as the true owner of the property. If the single-purpose corporation is the nominal owner of the property on behalf of the Canadian shareholder, or the corporation is deemed to be the owner on behalf of a shareholder, the IRS may ignore the corporation for estate tax purposes. Consequently, the shareholder of a single-purpose corporation may be exposed to the US estate tax, regardless of the corporate ownership of the property. The situation is worse for single-purpose corporations, because compliance with CRA guidelines (for property acquired prior to 2005) effectively causes the corporation to be viewed as a mere nominee of the shareholder.

You also have to remember that when a Canadian company owns property directly, the company will pay US corporate tax rates plus a branch tax of 5 percent.

Income Tax Issue

Owning US real estate through a corporation can significantly increase the income tax arising from the sale of US real estate. Current US federal tax law provides a maximum income tax rate of 15 percent on long-term *capital gains* (gains from the sale of capital assets held for at least twelve months). There are no preferential rates for capital gains recognized by a corporation. The federal corporate tax rate on such gains can be as high as 35 percent. Furthermore, some states impose a higher tax rate on gains of a corporation. For example, although Florida has no individual income tax, it imposes tax at a rate of 5.5 percent on corporations realizing capital gains on Florida real estate. Therefore, the federal and Florida tax rate on the sale of a Florida vacation home could exceed 40 percent if sold by a corporation, but would generally be limited to 15 percent if the home were sold by an individual.

Although these taxes may be less than the potential US estate tax, real estate investors need to weigh the ultimate cost of the Canadian corporate structure against the potential benefits. They must also consider the likelihood of selling the property prior to the investor's death.

Splitting Interest

Another technique to reduce exposure to US estate tax is to split interest ownership of the property. Under such an arrangement, an individual would acquire a life interest in US property and his or her children would acquire the remainder interest in the property. When the individual dies, there would be no estate tax on the life interest, since the life interest would have no value upon death. If the children die while holding a remainder interest, the estate tax would be assessed on the value of the remainder interest. Generally, the children can obtain term life insurance at low costs (because of their age) to protect them from estate tax exposure.

A split-interest arrangement usually involves a trust or partnership structure. The structure may be complex, but the tax savings may be worthwhile for certain family situations.

Obtaining Non-Recourse Debt Financing

A *non-recourse mortgage* outstanding on US real estate reduces the value of the property included in an individual's taxable estate. A non-recourse mortgage entitles the lender to have recourse only against the property mortgaged. If an individual defaults on payment, the mortgaged property can be seized, but there will be no further liability if the value of the property does not satisfy the debt.

Since most US lenders are reluctant to provide mortgages on a non-recourse basis, investors may need to find other sources of financing. One possible source of non-recourse financing is a spouse. Assume a wife has $100,000 to invest in a US vacation home. Instead of investing directly, she could loan her husband $100,000 on a non-recourse basis to acquire the property. Should he die, there will be no value in the estate, because the non-recourse debt from the value of the US property will be deducted. If she dies, there will be no value in the estate because the loan is not property situated in the United States. To be respected as true debt, the debt should have commercial characteristics, such as a market rate of interest and repayment terms.

This may create a problem, because the wife would have interest income for Canadian tax purposes and the husband would have no interest expense deduction. Because the US rules do not specify that the funds received from the mortgage must be used to acquire the US property, the husband might be able to acquire investment assets with the funds received. Acquiring additional assets may allow for a deductible carrying charge for Canadian tax purposes.

Another problem with non-recourse debt is that the debt does not change as the property appreciates. Consequently, should the property substantially appreciate in value and/or the principal of the debt be repaid, the debt will offset a smaller proportion of the value of the property.

Using a Partnership Structure

Although this is what insiders like to call an "unsettled area of law," you could argue that a Canadian partnership holding personal-use US property is not property situated in the US and, therefore, the Canadian partner is sheltered from US estate tax.

Another strategy is for the partnership to elect corporate status for US tax purposes. This makes the partnership a "foreign corporation" for US tax purposes and therefore exempt from US estate tax. To elect corporate status, the partnership must have some business activities beyond just holding personal-use real estate. One of the attractive features of this strategy is that, since the partnership will continue to be recognized as a partnership for Canadian tax purposes, the Canadian partner will not have a shareholder benefit (as this only applies to shareholders of a corporation). Unfortunately, because the partnership will be considered a corporation for US tax purposes, the tax arising from the sale of the property will not be eligible for the lower individual tax rates.

Under certain circumstances it may be possible to elect corporate status for US tax purposes after the partner's death. This will allow individual income tax rates on the sale of the property before death and provide insulation from the estate tax upon death. This is a complex strategy that requires extreme care to plan and implement.

REVIEW US ESTATE TAX PLANS

Although the Canada–US tax treaty reduces the US estate tax bite for many Canadians holding US property (generally those with total estates under US$5 million), it will not provide complete relief for larger estates.

Other issues for snowbirds include insurance. While a Canadian's insurance proceeds are not subject to US estate tax, the insurance proceeds can substantially increase the value of a decedent's estate at death and that could trigger US estate tax.

The final word about snowbirds and the US tax system echoes what accountants and lawyers on both sides of the border say: assess the impact of the US estate tax on your estate and seek professional help to put tax-mitigating strategies to work in Canada and the United States. At the same time, they also suggest that on top of a properly drafted will, estate planning should be considered well in advance of any purchases of US property. That makes estate planning (and US estate tax avoidance) part of a smart investor's early due diligence.

PART V
LEGAL PLANNING

36

The Three Pillars of Real Estate Asset Protection

There's a lot of debate about the differences between US and Canadian culture, but the US predilection for litigation always generates a great deal of talk. To an outsider, it may not appear that the two countries are that far apart, and at the very least, this appears to be one area where Canadians are catching up with their American cousins. In fact, it's the number one reason why property and liability insurance rates are climbing in both countries.

For example, in early 2010, an insurance company in Canada named a fourteen-year-old babysitter in a claim after a residential fire spread to a neighbor's property. The babysitter got the kids out of the dwelling, called the fire department, and alerted the neighbors. Her name was later dropped from the suit, but the brief media frenzy over the story gave a lot of Canadians new reasons to think about the potential liabilities associated with allowing their children to make a few extra dollars by babysitting.

Even though situations like this are becoming more commonplace in Canada, Canadian real estate investors are probably still unprepared for the litigious realities of doing business in the United States. Canadian investors certainly can expect to get a big lesson in what's considered "fair" if one of your business dealings ever ends up in a US court—the "fair" treatment doled out by American courts typically feels anything but fair!

A recent report by the US Chamber Institute for Legal Reform pointed to several states and counties where biased judges and juries are a known problem. That makes court decisions a real crapshoot in terms of the outcome you can expect. And a recent poll shows that three-quarters of all small-business owners in America expressed concern that they would be the target of an unfair lawsuit; six out of ten said the fear of lawsuits makes them feel more guarded about their business decisions; and 54 percent said lawsuits or the threat of lawsuits forced them to make decisions they ordinarily would not have made.

THE THREE PILLARS OF ASSET PROTECTION

Canadian real estate investors cannot expect to change the US legal system. Nor can they expect special treatment. They can, however, expect to improve their asset protection by following three core pillars of asset protection.

As you read through them, think about the areas where you may be vulnerable to problems. Take the following actions to protect your assets:

- Separate certain assets from yourself through title with entities.
- Insulate yourself with proper insurance and estate planning.
- Remove assets and equity from real property from harm's way by using global solutions or entities (e.g., trusts, limited liability companies, family limited partnerships).

KEY INSIGHT

Canadians investing in the US real estate market must accept that the legal system is not fair. There is no substitute for good legal advice.

LEARN WHAT ASSET PROTECTION IS AND ISN'T

There are a lot of misconceptions about US asset protection. Most come from misinformation shared by legal charlatans with unethical websites that discuss benefits that are not only illegal but also improbable.

Investors new to the US market need to know that asset protection does not involve the following activities:

- Evading tax
- Defrauding current creditors
- Hiding assets
- Rendering yourself insolvent

Asset protection in this market is about:

- Being strategic about placement of assets
- Protecting your assets

What does this mean? The strategic placement of assets aims to reduce liabilities and vulnerabilities, not to circumvent the law—it's all about being proactive. As an asset-protection-wise investor, you must implement the three pillars and separate (and sometimes remove) certain assets from yourself through title with entities or business structures (like the limited partnership or trusts). Having appropriate insurance and estate planning will also ensure that you and your companies are insulated from asset claims. These practices, adopted with the help of a legal and tax professional familiar with your business situation, provide some "distance" between your assets and your business liabilities.

The aim of protecting your assets is to level the litigation playing field. Since you can't rely on the US court system to always be fair, real estate investors must take care to protect their assets from litigation.

PERFORM DUE DILIGENCE

As we've discussed throughout this book, market opportunities abound in the US market. But there is no excuse for thinking you can check your due diligence strategies at the border!

While asset protection plans require the input of legal, tax, and insurance professionals, you should know about some key points regarding insurance and limited liability entities.

Proper Insurance

The kind of insurance you need will depend on your budget and what the industry considers your "insurable needs," i.e., how much insurance you need to protect your assets and your estate. Real estate investors should always fully investigate life and property insurance.

The amount of life insurance you need depends on two factors. One is the succession of capital to create a legacy, pay down taxes, and pay expenses. The other is *lifestyle capital*. This can be designed as a supplemental retired income–taking advantage of the tax code. The lifestyle capital would consider over-funding the policy beyond the insurance cost to build a tax-free cash value that the insured could take out as loans in the future.

You would not have "enough" insurance if your current coverage would not replace your income for a number of years, or cover the expenses of a larger estate. You can also consider it a way to create a tax-free legacy to your loved ones or a charity. The goal is to get the insurance when you are young and insurance is inexpensive, and lock in the pricing so that you can maximize the internal rate of return over the cost of the insurance.

Use of Limited Liability Entities

The exact structure you need to set up to protect your assets has to be decided on a case-by-case basis. At the very least, a person who owns property should want a basic asset protection plan that includes a limited liability entity—like a limited partnership or a limited liability limited partnership—to separate and control the asset, create some estate-planning options, and limit what the remedy creditors would have should they sue you for the value of the real property asset that is your investment.

KEY INSIGHT

Limited liability entities are not all equal. Canadians need to seek advice from a cross-border legal and tax specialist when setting one up. Canadians who set up a US limited liability company (LLC), for example, may leave themselves exposed to double taxation. A limited partnership offers some protection from liability and double taxation.

We give you more information about the tax implications of limited liability partnerships in Insight 33 about taking title in your US property investments. From an asset protection perspective, limited liability structures, coupled with adequate liability insurance, can provide some protection from liability arising from litigation relating to your property by restricting the claimant's reach to only those assets held by the partnership.

Use of Trusts/Land Trusts

Some commentators advocate using trusts or land trusts to protect your assets. The argument goes that by using a trust, your name is protected from any possible claimants in the event of a lawsuit. In fact, however, due diligence by the claimant's lawyer will quickly produce the names of the people behind the trust—land registries are required to divulge this information. So as a way to protect against litigious claimants, a trust may not be very effective.

37 Develop an Asset Protection Plan and Be Prepared to Avoid Lawsuits

The three pillars of asset protection from Insight 36 give you a sense of what you must do to protect your real estate investment wealth.

As a Canadian investing in US real estate, use these pillars to protect your US investments. You must also go into this market keenly aware that you are now doing business in one of the world's most litigious societies. How litigious? Drawing on some of the latest statistics, there were more than one million lawyers in the United States in 2006. Four years before that, 16 million civil cases were filed in state courts, according to the *State Court Guide to Statistical Reporting*. One year later, trial lawyers in the US earned an estimated $40 billion in lawsuit awards.

Even with a proactive asset protection plan, Canadians must enter this market fully aware that anyone who does business in the United States puts themselves at risk of legal action. In fairness, another statistic from the Bureau of Justice Statistics shows that in 1995, 97 percent of US legal cases were terminated before they went to trial. This statistic holds relatively true in 2012 and most cases never make it to trial. But if you think that sounds like good news, think again. Not everyone who files a civil lawsuit intends to fight it through to its legal conclusion. Some litigants may be motivated by the opportunity to cost you money and to make you and your business "disappear" from a certain market. Never forget that it takes real money to fight a civil action—no matter how frivolous—and it can take almost as much money to *prepare* to fight a civil action that is eventually terminated.

The situation is not any better if you are the plaintiff in a legal action. While anyone can file a civil lawsuit in the United States for any reason, it is much harder to win a case. As mentioned in Insight 33, the US court system isn't always fair.

Here are four hair-raising examples of real US legal cases to help you understand the kind of legal environment you will be working in when you invest in US real estate. Rest assured that a lot of Canadian real estate investors will never encounter a lawsuit while doing business in the United States, but you always must be prepared for what could happen in this litigious environment.

CASE 1: THE VEXATIOUS LITIGANT

One Seattle woman made headlines because she had forty-five lawsuits going on simultaneously. She is what's called a *vexatious litigant*. That's a person who brings legal action to harass or subdue an opponent. Vexatious litigants typically launch frivolous lawsuits or file repetitive grievances not based on the merits of a situation. These individuals may be motivated by malice and the desire to annoy or embarrass an adversary.

Some states have a statute against this kind of activity and some do not. Regardless, be aware of the people you encounter and be prepared to question their motivations.

An ounce of prevention is worth a pound of cure.

CASE 2: THE CYCLIST

A man was riding his bike at night. It was equipped with reflectors but not lights, and he was hit by a vehicle. The cyclist was awarded $6 million because he maintained he was not warned that reflectors might not be enough to prevent an accident. The takeaway message is remarkably loud and clear: you are not protected from someone else's ignorance. (Indeed, you can't use ignorance as your defense, either!)

Review the biggest threats to your wealth in Insight 38.
If something concerns you, prepare for it.

CASE 3: THE TOPPLING TODDLER

An American woman was awarded $700,000 when she tripped over a toddler who was running in a furniture store. The crux of this case did not rest on the extent of the woman's injuries, nor did it matter that the toddler she tripped over was her own child. Instead, the business responsible for the space where the mishap occurred had to pay a significant settlement for a mishap that arguably resulted from the injured woman's own negligence.

You think this is ridiculous? It doesn't matter what you think!
What matters is that you know what could happen and
you take steps in advance to protect yourself.

CASE 4: THE WEEKEND GETAWAY

In another case that defies what some might view as a common-sense approach to legal jurisprudence, a man was awarded $500,000 after he was trapped in someone else's garage for a weekend. The successful litigant had broken into the home. He sued for emotional distress because there was only dog food to eat and Coca-Cola to drink. (In fairness, he was trapped for the whole weekend!)

Again, it's not about what you think. It's about
what you know might happen.

STAY OUT OF COURT BY BEING PREPARED

The advice here boils down to one salient point: lawsuits threaten your assets. Develop an asset protection plan and make sure you are as prepared as you can be to avoid a lawsuit. Pay particular attention to the threats identified in Insight 38 and never forget that you are now doing business in a country whose legal system does not appear to value personal responsibility (or common sense) when weighing the claims of plaintiffs in civil lawsuits to the same level as Canada does.

KEY INSIGHT

These warnings and statistics show that Canadian real estate investors should avoid getting caught up in the American legal system. Once you are in that court system, anything can happen.

38

Counter Threats to Your Wealth with Foresight

When Canadian investors are asked what constitutes the biggest threat to their US real estate investment wealth, many worry about mistakenly buying properties that are not a good fit with their investment strategies. In other words, they are concerned about making a poor investment choice based on misinformation from a relative stranger. As an extension of that worry, they also fear that a US investment could turn sour and put their Canadian assets at risk if a legal liability were to occur. (And they are right—a US judgment can go after your Canadian wealth.)

Well, there's good news and bad news. The good news is that proper due diligence offers some real protection against buying the wrong properties. It also helps you identify those times when you need to revise an exit strategy. (Noticing market changes may lead you to sell a property you had purchased to buy and hold, for example.)

In addition, due diligence can help you set up the appropriate asset protection for your US enterprise, from arranging a particular corporate structure, to increasing your insurance coverage, putting an equity reduction plan in place, and keeping a Canadian bank account.

The bad news is that some of the most significant threats to your real estate investment wealth come from problems you can't necessarily solve with that kind of due diligence. You can adopt and practice "the best" business strategies and "the best" asset protection plans, but those actions won't necessarily protect you from a legal blindside. That's because, believe it or not, some of the most significant threats to your wealth will come (quite unexpectedly) from people you know—and sometimes from people you know really well!

This does not mean you should be too wary to invest. But it does mean you must always be realistic about how your real estate investments could be affected by influences far beyond your portfolio. As a Canadian real estate investor, understand that when it comes to doing business in the US market, your first rule of thumb should always be *protect yourself*.

Zero in on protecting the following three areas:

- Your business

- Your personal life, including accidents and other unforeseeable events

- Your investment properties

KEY INSIGHT

If this list makes you think that you have to be watchful in *all* aspects of your life, you're right!

Unfortunately, an all-inclusive list such as this won't necessarily help you decrease your liability exposure because, believe it or not, it's way too logical. But start thinking about all of the what-if scenarios that could hurt the wealth associated with your business, your personal life, or your investment properties in case of a lawsuit. This kind of forward thinking can be a little scary, but it is essential.

We hope the list of the top threats to your wealth (see the next section) helps you to see the importance of continually reviewing your business, personal life, and investment properties. Habitually look for potentially problematic areas where you need to update your approach to wealth protection.

KEY INSIGHT

Canadian investors will find themselves in a far more litigious business environment as soon as they start buying property in the United States. Start making "what-if" questions a staple of your business decision-making process, then take action to decrease your exposure to legal action.

THE TOP THREATS TO YOUR WEALTH

Here are the biggest threats to your wealth:

- **Your own physical or mental incapacity and the need for nursing care:** What happens to the business or investment portfolio if you do not have disability insurance? Does your plan include a way for other business partners/family members to step in and carry on?

- **Divorce:** No one wants to think about how the dissolution of a marriage could affect an investment portfolio or a business, but you do need a plan that establishes shared assets and liabilities. If it's necessary to buy a domestic partner out, you may need to sell all of your assets.

- **A business liability:** You don't have time to establish a workable plan that protects every aspect of your business from a potential liability. Talk to your lawyer and establish a good rapport with an insurance professional. As your business changes, so will your liability exposure. Be prepared.

- **Tenants:** Yes, you can be sued if a tenant gets injured, even if the tenant's activity caused the safety issue, so keep your properties well maintained, carry property insurance, and make sure your tenants know they are responsible for insuring their belongings. In many cases, all parties, including the insurance company that provides insurance over the property, could be held liable for problems on a particular property. But the landlord is ultimately responsible, meaning that you need regular property insurance plus an umbrella policy that covers things beyond the normal policy.

- **Accidents:** Realize that courts will often deem "accidents" to have been preventable. Keep your properties well maintained and make sure your liability insurance is adequate. What's adequate for someone else may not be adequate for you and your business, so seek specific advice.

- **Trespassing on your property:** You can be held liable for injuries to someone who is on your property illegally! Again, be prepared for the what-ifs. Quality property maintenance is key, but you still need liability insurance to protect your assets.

- **Worker injury on your property:** Just like the message of the last three points, you can be held responsible when bad things happen on your property.

- **Ownership of animals that might harm someone:** Again, plan for what-ifs—even for animals your tenants own.

If some of these items gave you pause for second thought, that's good. You must always act as though some of the most significant economic perils to your business interests lurk where the naïve investor least expects. So don't be naïve. Try to do the following:

- **Anticipate problems before they arise.** Conduct regular property inspections, keep maintenance and repairs up to date, and ensure your rental property is being taken care of.

- **Plan for the what-ifs.** Talk to your insurer about changes to your business that could affect your coverage level. Work with your lawyer and tax accountant to plan asset protection contingencies that cover changes to your personal and professional situation.

- **Get advice before you need it.** A proactive approach to asset protection means seeking quality advice often. Let your legal, tax, and insurance professionals know you take asset protection seriously and want their help.

- **Learn from your mistakes and the mistakes of others.** Be a student of your industry. Follow up on good ideas you hear from other investors. Develop a best practice model for how your business operates.

39

Draw Up a Blueprint for Your Estate Plan

Nearly all of the real estate investors we've met over the years understand that they are in business to make money. Many of them have a basic understanding of the importance of asset protection and the fact that asset protection is an even greater concern if you're doing business in the United States, given the litigious disposition of that business environment. What an amazing number of these investors do not understand is the critical role that estate planning plays in terms of long-term asset protection.

No one likes to think about dying, but that fear doesn't make dying any less of a possibility. It does, however, get in the way of your ability to ensure that your hard-earned assets make it into the hands of the people you have chosen to control those assets after you die.

KEY INSIGHT

Real estate investors who seek help to design a solid estate plan are proving that they know what long-term asset protection is all about.

Here's an overview of the basic information you need to know as you set up an estate plan.

PROBATE

Probate is the legal process that kicks into action after someone dies. It means that the court and legal system step in to interpret the terms of your will. If you have a well-written will that clearly lays out what you want to happen, then the will is administered accordingly. If you die *intestate* (meaning without having written a will), the legal system will use a statutory scheme to distribute your belongings to your next of kin. Your loved ones will share your property in the way that the state deems to be fair, but it can turn into a battlefield where families play tug-of-war for your assets. By not preparing a will, you not only give up any say as to who gets what upon your death, you may leave problems for your beloved at a time when they are having to cope with their loss and grief. You should consult a lawyer to make sure that your will reflects your wishes.

We'll talk a bit more about probate later, but the most important point to remember for now is that estate planning is massively important to anyone with assets. Your passing will be hard enough for your relatives and business partners; don't make it even more difficult by exposing your estate to lawsuits, probate fees, and other costs.

KEY INSIGHT

If you want to protect your loved ones and make sure your assets are distributed according to your wishes, you need an estate plan.

ADOPT A PLAN

A good estate plan will go far to ensuring that your estate can be wound up quickly and efficiently by your nominated executor, and that your assets are distributed according to your wishes for protecting your loved ones and managing ongoing investments.

Without an estate plan, and in particular a will appointing an executor, your estate could be frozen while the legalities of appointing an administrator, and any disagreements amongst your heirs about this, are sorted out, entailing unnecessary costs. In addition, a good estate plan prevents unnecessary drains on your assets to pay probate fees, where some assets can be sheltered from that process. The elements of a good estate plan are departure documents, incapacity issues, and planning for tax and probate.

Departure Documents

Departure documents come into play upon your death and they are essential to the probate process. They include trusts and wills.

Trusts

A *trust* is really an agreement between you and someone you've assigned to manage your assets. Title to your assets is transferred to the trust, which is managed by the trustee. You are no longer the owner of those assets. In the trust you will also direct what is to happen to these assets on your death, and who will benefit. This allows you to avoid probate on these assets. At the creation of the trust when you transfer assets to the trust, there is a deemed disposition and the trust acquires them at fair market value and you will pay capital gains tax. When you die, there is no probate required. If you want to include American assets in the trust, American tax laws will apply and accordingly you should obtain American tax advice for this aspect of the transaction.

Will

A *will* simply names the people who will receive your assets upon your death. When crafting a will, you'll need to nominate an *executor*. This individual will manage and distribute your estate, in addition to paying any outstanding debts and settling accounts. In your will, you also will name the guardians for your children should they be under age upon your death. Remember, only assets in your name will be subject to your will. In Canada, a will should be signed by you in front of two witnesses.

Incapacity Issues

The second layer of the base plan is designed to deal with *incapacity issues*—when people are still alive but have been rendered incapable of making decisions on their own, because of traumatic injury, stroke, or any other frailty that could arise. (These concepts may have different names in Canada and can even differ from province to province. Always get good legal advice.)

Continuing Power of Attorney

A *power of attorney* is a legal document that authorizes another person to act on your behalf. This should not be confused with an executor, who has been authorized to carry out the provisions of a will. Unless you limit your attorney's authority, they can do almost anything with your property that you could do—such as act for you in financial dealings, banking, or in buying and selling property. You might choose to limit the power of attorney for a specific time period, such as when you are away on holiday.

A general power of attorney is only effective while you are mentally sound. The moment you become mentally incapacitated, the power of attorney ceases. A *continuing power of attorney* for property, however, lets your attorney act for you in the event you become mentally incapable of managing your property. To be valid for this purpose, the document must either be called a continuing power of attorney, or clearly state that it gives your attorney the power to continue acting for you if you become mentally incapable. This will mean that your family member, or whomever you have appointed as attorney, doesn't have to go to court to manage your affairs.

KEY INSIGHT

Get your continuing power of attorney in place. When domestic partners or others go in on real estate together, it is always recommended that the partners prepare a plan that goes into action should one of them be incapacitated. Without having a continuing power of attorney, you would have no authority to get things done with the property, including selling it, should something untoward happen to your partner.

Power of Attorney for Personal Care

You can give someone a *power of attorney for personal care*, which allows them to make decisions on your behalf with respect to your health care, medical treatment, housing, clothing, and safety. The existence or absence of a power of attorney for personal care has generated a lot of news in recent years, as high-profile cases have seen families battle over the health-care decisions of loved ones. This means that doctors can get consent to treatment from your attorney as a substitute decision-maker in the event that you are mentally incapacitated by disease or accident. It also means that you can set out your wishes with respect to medical procedures that you may not want to allow. Having a health-care directive ensures that someone you've chosen will have the power to decide whether to accept or decline health measures on your behalf, should you become incapacitated.

Without one of these documents, lengthy legal battles can arise in the case of medical incapacity.

Other Considerations

Probate

When people die with a will, probate must be filed with the courts in each jurisdiction where the estate has assets. There are filing and legal fees involved, which can be 5 percent or more of the value of the estate, depending on where the assets are located. If you die without a will, or *intestate*, then the courts and lawyers have to get involved to appoint administrators of the estate, which incurs more costs and delays for your estate, especially if the process is contested.

There are some ways to get assets outside of the probate process. In Canada, for example, where you name beneficiaries to a life insurance policy, those funds can pass directly to the beneficiaries without going through probate. In addition, where property is held as *joint tenants* (between spouses for example), the property will automatically pass to the surviving joint tenant without being added to the value of the estate that is subject to probate. This also applies with life estates. This compares with the situation where you hold your property solely in your name (fee simple) and the value of the property is subject to the probate process.

Structure the ownership of your property to reduce probate costs

There are legal structures that you can employ to avoid probate and the costs associated with that process. If all your assets are transferred either on or before your death, you can avoid probate. While it's unlikely that you will be able to transfer all of your assets before your death, you can deal with your property this way. One of the most usual ways to do this, especially when owning real estate, is by way of joint tenancy with the right of survivorship.

Joint tenancy with the right of survivorship

You and your spouse, or any two people, may hold title as joint tenants with the right of survivorship. The survivors are usually named as the children of the parents. Upon the death of the first person, title in the property automatically transfers to the surviving spouse whose name is on the title deed. Upon the death of the surviving party, the property, again by law, is transferred to the named survivors, normally the children.

The transfers take place outside your will, and as a result, there is no requirement for probate.

Depending on the net worth of the owners, US estate tax can apply.

Life estate

Another common method of holding title to real estate is by way of a *life estate* with the remainder normally going to your children. As long as you are alive, you hold the property (hence the name life estate). When you die, the property is automatically transferred to the people who are named as the *remaindermen*. Again, because you do not hold the property on your death, there is no need for probate, and also, in this case, there is no estate tax payable.

Community property with the right of survivorship

Married couples in certain jurisdictions, for example Arizona and California, can hold title as community property with the right of survivorship. The survivors, normally the children, are named in the deed. Upon the death of the first spouse, as with joint tenancy, the property transfers by operation of law to the surviving spouse, and upon that person's death, to those named as survivors. This structure is similar in effect to that of a joint tenancy with right of survivorship. Again, there is no probate, but, depending on the net worth of the owners, US estate tax can apply.

Beneficiary deed

In certain states, property can be held by way of a *beneficiary deed*. These are "transfer on death" deeds, where your beneficiaries can be named in a signed deed or affidavit. This document is filed with the title-recording office, and the property can be transferred by presenting the death certificate there. Again, probate is avoided, but depending on the value of the estate, tax can apply. The states where you can hold property with a beneficiary deed are Arizona, Arkansas, Colorado, Indiana, Kansas, Michigan, Minnesota, Missouri, Montana, Nevada, New Mexico, Ohio, Oklahoma, and Wisconsin.

Tenants in common

If there are two or more of you, normally where you are not related, you can hold the property as *tenants in common*. With this structure, you can define what proportion of the property each person holds. For example, two partners can hold the property as 50-50 partners, or some other proportion, perhaps to reflect how much money each put into the purchase. On the death of one of the owners, his proportion of the property would pass to his estate, which would have to go through probate, and then would be passed on in accordance with his will. Estate tax can apply, depending on the net worth of the estate.

Trusts

A trust can own property as well and the terms of the trust will determine what happens in terms of probate. The legal effects are based upon the terms of the trust. Probate should not apply. Normally it is not a good idea to register title in the name of the trust, because on resale the purchaser will require confirmation that all of the terms of the trust have been complied with and this could cause legal issues on the resale. To avoid this situation one person or a corporation could be the registered owner as nominee for the trust. Depending on the net worth of the owners, US estate tax can apply.

Estate Tax

Canada, unlike the United States, does not have an estate tax. Nevertheless, estate tax could affect Canadians who own US real estate (or other US assets). To find out how it might affect your US assets, Canadians must talk to a cross-border tax specialist.

In Canada, there is no estate tax, but there is a deemed disposition on death, which can result in capital gains tax being payable. Capital gains tax, however, is not as punitive as estate tax. See Insight 35 for more information on estate tax.

KEY INSIGHT

Do not allow ordinary events to undo your asset protection plan. Risk management always includes an estate plan.

40

Steer Clear of Asset Protection Fakes, Scams, and Planning Errors

Canadians who are thinking about investing in US real estate are wise to take asset protection seriously. You need to be especially wary of anyone who tries to tell you there is such a thing as "complete" asset protection or a bulletproof asset protection plan. These do not exist.

Insight 11 in Part 2 of this book addresses the variety of scams that can put your assets at risk as soon as you try to enter the distressed property market. The essential message there is that there will always be individuals and groups trying to take your money under the guise of helping you make money. That doesn't change as your portfolio grows and you have more assets to protect.

So first and foremost, run from anything that purports to offer complete asset protection or bulletproof asset protection. It's likely a scam. If you do try to pursue a problem arising from this kind of scam through the US court system, the issue will likely never make it to trial. There, your real goal will be some sort of settlement. So at that point, the best course of action would be to make sure you have the legal advice you need to exert some input over what those settlement figures would be.

This Insight looks at some areas that you should be extremely cautious about getting into.

LAND TRUSTS

Investors who spend any time on the real estate seminar circuit likely will find themselves at a seminar that promotes the land trust as a way of avoiding personal liability—a kind of silver-bullet protection against lawsuits. We're here to tell you that it's not.

A *land trust* is a special trust ownership structure that enables the owner of real property to place the legal ownership of that property in the name of a trustee. This arrangement, which is not allowed in every US state, is a way to keep confidential the names of the "true owners" of the property. Once real property has been transferred to a land trust, the owner maintains only an "interest" in the trust, which is administered under personal property laws, not real estate laws.

Under US law, there are two types of trusts: revocable and irrevocable. The irrevocable trust can give some protection against litigation. It also comes with significant handcuffs, since an irrevocable trust enables you to gift the asset into the trust, but once this is done you no longer have control over the asset. This would mean you cannot sell or liquidate the asset and that an independent third-party trustee must oversee all transactions on behalf of the trust. Without those provisions, the irrevocability of the trust would be considered a sham.

The land trust is effectively the same as a living or revocable trust. It is a revocable trust, or an agreement you can revoke or amend during your lifetime. It becomes irrevocable only upon death, when it sets out how your assets will be allocated. From that perspective, it has real value in an estate plan.

The land trust is a legitimate way to place real property into a governance arrangement. In the real estate investment world, however, extra caution is warranted when dealing with a land trust. Whereas the arrangement is sometimes marketed as a de facto means to protect your assets, the only thing the land trust accomplishes is getting title out of your own name. It will not protect the asset from a committed attorney who is out to collect on behalf of a client for an injury connected with the property.

In many states, including Arizona, you must disclose all trustees and beneficiaries of a land trust. If you are trying to use the land trust for asset protection, you likely will want to be on the list of beneficiaries so that you can have at least some input into the trust. As soon as you do that, however, you leave yourself exposed to a future liability related to that trust. Think of it as a win-win scenario—with a recognizable potential to morph quickly into a lose-lose situation.

Generally speaking, you would want to set up your US land trust as what is referred to as *self-settled*, which is a special needs trust that's funded with property that belongs to the beneficiary. This is only allowed in a few states, so you must be mindful of what's possible in the state where you are doing business. Indeed, most states disallow such a transaction and will not provide any protection to the investor for a liability connected to their real estate. Again, know your options and get good advice specific to your situation.

LIMITED LIABILITY COMPANIES

Whereas a limited partnership may offer Canadians some asset protection via limited liability and avoid double taxation, a *limited liability company* (LLC) usually spells trouble. In an LLC, the owners and managers are given a "limited liability." That is, they receive some protection against being held personally responsible for the financial debts and obligations of a company should those debts and obligations not be met. Typically, their losses cannot exceed the amount they invested.

For American citizens, an LLC is a great protection tool under most circumstances. It helps their estates avoid probate and offers tax benefits for an appreciating asset. For Canadians, however, the limited liability protection is generally not enough to make a US LLC a good idea, because the US LLC can leave you vulnerable to double taxation!

Like all business transactions, this is an area that should be examined closely by an advisor with good cross-border experience. By default, you must be cautious when dealing with people who insist the LLC is always an option for your real estate holdings and a good vehicle for asset protection.

UNDERSTAND YOUR STRATEGY: PROBATE VERSUS CREDIT PROTECTION

People must be clear about the type of protection they're getting when they opt for different structures. Is it protection from *probate*, which is the court process to decide distribution of a deceased's property, or is it protection against creditors? Many times the planning may be exclusive, that is, the provisions you put in place for probate protection (like a good will and estate plan) may have little effect on creditor protection, for which you will need completely different strategies. Again, this makes advice specific to your circumstances absolutely essential.

KEY INSIGHT

If you're looking for asset protection advice, take a pass on the kind that comes to you via a series of CDs you have to buy and listen to. What you really need is advice based on your situation. "Thinking" you have asset protection is not the same as having it! Your business goal is to protect your assets from lawsuits. This is not an area where it makes sense to do it yourself.

OFFSHORE TRUSTS AND IBCs

Sometimes investors are sold on very expensive offshore trusts or international business companies (IBCs). When transferred into these entities improperly, you risk cataclysmic tax consequences regardless of whether you are a Canadian or American citizen. Here the issue is the perceived ownership of a foreign entity. The Supreme Court of Canada recently ruled that offshore trusts or IBCs, where the mind, management, and control are with a Canadian taxpayer, notwithstanding the structure and terms of the trust, are taxable entities.

HOMESTEAD EXEMPTION

The same goes for investment deals that try to talk up the *homestead exemption*. Homestead exemptions are found in state statutes and US constitutional provisions. They exist to protect the value of residents' homes from property taxes, creditors, and circumstance that might arise from the death of a homeowner spouse. Be aware, however, that these generally do not apply to investment properties and are meant for limited use with your own personal residence.

KEY INSIGHT

It really doesn't matter whether you're buying investment real estate in Canada or the US. Your team must include good legal and tax advisors and you must be careful about acting on any advice that hasn't been vetted through a legal and tax specialist. Many of the people you meet in real estate investment do want to help you make money. Good advisors will help you keep it.

TRANSFERRING ASSETS TO FAMILY MEMBERS

In Canada and the United States, individuals facing a pending lawsuit often look for ways to transfer their assets into the names of family members. It is a bad strategy on both sides of the border because a court will examine the substance over the form.

Courts in the United States are adamant that you must be able to demonstrate an *arm's-length transaction*; therefore, if you have sold an asset, there should be a transfer of funds. When it comes to the transfer of property, the courts will, in all likelihood, determine that it is not reasonable that a person would make such a substantial gift to another person. The court is especially likely to dismiss such a transaction if the transfer frustrates a creditor who has won a judgment. Indeed, the court may order that this kind of transfer be unwound or returned so that the asset or proceeds can be delivered to the creditor.

KEY INSIGHT

Courts will bring hindsight to bear on an investor's actions. This is why your asset protection plan needs to be in place before or as you buy real estate, not after a deal is done. As with everything in your investment life, steer clear of taking quick action on "foolproof" strategies. If a deal is being sold as "too good to last," make sure your due diligence investigates whether it's "too good to be true."

PART VI

CROSS-BORDER BANKING AND FINANCING

41

Understand Cross-Border Issues

Forewarned is forearmed, so the goal of this Insight is to provide a little more practical information about how issues like citizenship, insurance, and finding joint venture investment partners can affect your US residential real estate investment decisions.

OVERCOME YOUR CITIZENSHIP ISSUES

Before we get into what some Canadians would consider to be among the grittier topics associated with US real estate investment, we take a broader look at cross-border issues. Insights 15 and 42 tackle the problems Canadians encounter when seeking to acquire financing from US lenders. Let's have a look now at what's behind those problems and give you some ideas about how you might alleviate them by paying a little extra attention to your immigration status.

First, rest assured that when it comes to buying US property, Canadians have the same legal rights as American citizens, so there are no barriers to a Canadian who wants to buy a residential property in the United States. But virtually every American lender will ask about your immigration status, and your ability to get US financing will be impaired or eliminated if all you have is temporary status as a tourist or businessperson and you are not a US citizen or a permanent resident with a green card.

To be clear, the green card attests to the *permanent* resident status of an alien in the United States. (This is completely different from the *temporary* status afforded by the basic business or tourist visa Canadians can get at the border crossing.) *Green card* also refers to the immigration process you follow to become a permanent US resident, and from the conventional US lender's perspective, this policy is in place to protect them from being burned by foreign nationals or delays with immigration processing.

KEY INSIGHT

Without citizenship or a permanent resident green card, Canadians will likely be required to put down at least 30 percent on any loans they acquire from a conventional US lender, if they can get one at all.

There are a few, relatively simple things Canadians can do to work around these rules. For example, you can buy residential real estate property through a company to which lenders may feel more comfortable lending money. Another strategy is to provide a copy of your immigration paper-work upfront if you are a US citizen, have applied, or are in the process of applying for a green card, or have a work visa such as an E-2 or a Trade NAFTA (TN) visa under the North American Free Trade Agreement (NAFTA). (E-2 and TN visas are discussed later in this Insight.) Some lenders accept a copy of the visa plate pasted into your passport or the card stapled to the passport as evidence of your immigration status, even though it merely confirms you are not a US citizen or a permanent resident.

Other Canadians experience some success by presenting a lender with US tax returns showing US income earned in the United States; this also could help convince a US lender of your intent to repay your loan. If your US deals are contingent on American financing, you also may want to talk to your lawyer about pursuing more complicated strategies. As always, where there is a will, there is a way.

You'll want to keep in mind the following three practical considerations when you grapple with the decisions you'll need to make when you conduct cross-border business and face issues related to citizenship.

Make Honesty Your Only Policy

With all the interest in US residential real estate investment, a lot of Canadians are entering the US on fact-finding missions. They're going into the United States for a closer look at the market, but may or may not buy property. When asked the reason for your entry into the United States, you could tell border authorities that you are entering the county "on business" and say that you are "going to talk about real estate" if asked for more information. You do not have to say you are looking at distressed property or foreclosures.

If you've entered the United States on a pleasure trip and find a property you want to buy as an investment, you can make an offer on the property. Just remember that you may not qualify for US financing. Until Canadian or US financing is in place, be careful what you promise.

KEY ISSUE

The central issue with US financing appears to be plain old-fashioned xenophobia, based on concerns about establishing identity and possible fraud, as well as problems of enforcement in the event of default. This is less personal than systemic, so never think you can "talk your way" past anyone, from border authorities to bankers. As always, aim to work within the system and make honesty your only policy.

Consider Getting a Green Card

If US financing is a deal breaker, or becomes a deal breaker as you grow your US investment portfolio, you may want to consider getting a green card. But be careful. A green card exposes Canadians to US tax on world-wide income. That's right. Profits from any of your Canadian businesses may be taxable then in the United States.

And there are other implications, too. Under current law, all male US citizens must register with Selective Service, including those who hold a green card, which signals permanent resident status. The Selective Service System maintains information on citizens potentially subject to military conscription.

For more information about green cards and immigration processes, please visit the US Citizenship and Immigration Services website at www.uscis.gov.

Perform Cross-Border Management

Although it can be very complicated to manage US properties from Canada, there may not be any legal issues related to managing a US port-folio from north of the 49th parallel if your "work" involves collecting rents or hiring contractors (plumbers and other tradespeople) to complete upgrades and repairs.

That changes if US customs officials get the impression that you are doing things that deprive US citizens of jobs. This is more likely to be a problem when you are managing multiple properties. If this is an issue, you should explore an E-2 visa or TN (treaty nations) work permit.

Available only to "treaty nations" (which includes Canada), the *E-2 visa* allows individuals to enter and work in the United States based on an investment they control inside the United States. This visa is renewable in three-year increments so long as the applicant remains in business.

Under NAFTA, Canadians also can apply for a work permit at a port of entry. To qualify for a *TN work permit*, you need to enter the US to work in a profession listed in NAFTA.

ACQUIRING AN E-2 VISA OR TN WORK PERMIT

To be eligible for a TN work permit, you must hold a university degree in the field in which you plan to work in the United States, have a valid passport, be able to show proof of employment, and seek TN designation for a profession recognized by NAFTA. Experience may be required in addition to a degree and some professions list an alternative to a university degree.

For a detailed list of professions, go to www.consular.canada.usembassy.gov/nafta_professions.asp.

If you are university educated and want to pursue a TN designation to qualify your US immigration status, talk to a cross-border lawyer about how you might qualify under one of the listed professions.

For more information on how to acquire an E-2 visa or TN work permit, visit www.travel.state.gov/visa.

If your immigration status is holding you back, enlist the help of a cross-border legal specialist.

42

Familiarize Yourself with US Mortgage Financing

Insight 15 reviews the complications of getting a US bank to loan Canadians money to buy US investment real estate. We will reiterate some of the key points about private financing and hard-money lenders, because the US loan process is relatively simple if you want to buy a second home, and that's what many Canadian real estate investors would like to do while they're doing business.

First, the large and stable lenders in the United States are more than happy to provide second-home mortgages for Canadians. The typical down payment required in the United States is 20 to 35 percent and interest rates are usually 0.25 or 0.5 percent above the rate for US nationals.

LOAN APPLICATION

To apply for a mortgage in the United States you need to have all of your financial papers in order. At the beginning of the process, the bank will request:

- T4 slips from the last two years and your last two pay stubs
- T1 returns for the last two years
- Your most recent 60-day history of checking and savings accounts and all RRSP statements or any other investments that you own
- A list of your lines of credit, with balances available
- Your most recent mortgage statement or rent receipt

- A copy of your tax bill for all real estate owned (to verify the tax amount)

- A list of vehicle payments

- Your social insurance number (to check your credit history)

- Legible copies of your passport

The bank will pull your Canadian credit history and arrive at a score. The score required to proceed with the loan differs by institution. There are two Canadian credit reporting agencies that you can contact to check your rating: Equifax Canada (www.equifax.ca) and TransUnion (www.tuc.ca).

It takes some time to gather all the information, but buyers who take all of this data to their first meetings will find it greatly expedites the process.

> Check your own credit score before you borrow money. It's not uncommon for problems with a credit score to be related to issues with mistaken identity or situations you could explain. Clean up these issues before they're used against you.

US LOAN APPLICATION TIPS

- Use a black pen on all documents that are being faxed or scanned.

- Expect your interest rate to fluctuate until you have a property under contract, because this is how the American system works.

- At the very end of the full approval process, just before the deal closes, you will need to act quickly to meet the bank's deadlines. All documents and passports must be notarized and couriered back to the title company within a 24-hour period. Anticipate this time crunch and leave a day free to get this done.

- Apply for a US checking account and credit card through your US bank after the mortgage is approved or when you next are in the United States. The credit card will not be a regular credit card because you do not have established credit in the United States. You will be able to use it like a debit card to access cash or cover incidentals. This is a great way to build your US credit history a little more quickly.

INVESTOR LOANS

A few US institutions will provide investor loans for Canadians. These will have higher interest rates and down payment requirements than a second-home loan. To reiterate points from Insight 15, your investor financing options likely will occur outside the traditional banking system. Here are some of your options.

Private Financing

This money is backed by individuals or organizations that lend to investors. They will check your credit and review your portfolio, but may be willing to work with a lower credit score than would be required by a traditional lender. The down payment is usually 25 to 30 percent and interest rates hover around 10 to 12 percent. Also, expect a one-time up-front fee of 1 to 3 percent of the loan.

Hard-Money Lenders

Hard-money lenders are private investors who focus on the value of the property. These are really asset-based loans, so the borrower's credit score is not important. Some auction lenders will lend within twenty-four hours, but it normally takes a week because they won't lend before a property has been properly inspected. Hard-money lenders will lend up to 70 percent of the purchase price. Interest rates are usually between 15 and 18 percent and the setup fee is between 1 and 5 percent. Investors use this for bridge financing and for fix-and-flip projects.

PROCEED WITH CAUTION!

Understand what you're getting into. The hard-money lending pool teems with sharks. Remember, this loan isn't about believing in you, it's about believing in your property. These lenders have taken a close look at your property and know they can make their money back if they have to take back the property for non-payment of the loan. It's not uncommon for hard-money lenders to want all of their money back within 12 months.

Investors who want to swim in this pool must be very careful. The fix-and-sell market is tough. If you've borrowed heavily to buy and renovate a property and it doesn't sell, you could lose both the property and your cash.

---

43 Buy US Real Estate Property with Other People's Money

If you've looked at some of the issues in Insight 42, it's easy to see that financing US real estate investment property with funds from US institutions is complicated if you live north of the 49th parallel. Some Canadian investors will avoid all of the potential hassles by using their own money to finance their first properties. Others will bring in other investors who have money to invest, but no inclination to do the work. In the real estate investment business, when they work together that's called a *joint venture deal*.

Canadian real estate and joint venture guru Don R. Campbell says that in a joint venture deal, one partner (you) finds the deal and has the expertise to make it work, while another partner or partners puts up all or part of the cash in return for the investment opportunity. Many Canadian investors use a 50-50 co-venture to acquire real estate where one person is the money partner and the other the property expert. The money partner lets the property expert handle the day-to-day operations associated with running the business.

Bringing other people's money into your real estate deals opens a lot of great opportunities for Canadian investors who want to use that money to leverage their own funds and expertise. To really make this process work, you've got to pay even closer attention to your due diligence and make sure you're buying into the "right deal." This is critical because a successful deal is the best way to attract even more funds to your investment business.

KEY INSIGHT

Nothing screams "Success!" like a real estate investment deal that makes money for you and your partners. Co-venturers who see their investments pay off are more likely to increase their investment and send other investors your way.

Beyond sticking to sound real estate fundamentals that help you acquire cash-flowing buy-and-hold properties with long-term equity appreciation, you want to pay close attention to *who* you bring into your deals. In particular, you must understand that:

- You cannot work with everyone.
- You do not have to work with everyone.

The argument is simple. The US market for distressed property is hot, and while Canadians are aware there is money to be made, a lot of them do not know how to do it. For that reason, savvy Canadian real estate investors who view the US foreclosures market as ripe for the picking can become what the industry calls "money magnets" if they can show other people that their investments make money. If that's what you want to do, you also must be able to show less-well-informed potential investors that you know *why* your investments work—and that's why you are in charge. For example, you can show them how you find deeply discounted properties and then renovate them efficiently, effectively, and economically; buy properties in areas with strong rental demand and a rising market for first-time homebuyers; and keep your units rented. All this shows investors you can put their money to work in the same way.

KEY INSIGHT

Showing what you have done already is a good way to show potential investors what you plan to do in the future.

BEGIN WITH PEOPLE YOU KNOW

Being able to attract co-venture money does not mean you must bring into your deals all of the money that comes your way. This is very important because it can make or break your business.

Don R. Campbell tells us that he structures his co-venture deals to make sure that both parties win when the deal works out, but during the process he maintains control of the deal and the decisions made around it. This approach puts the investor—who's doing the work—in charge.

He's also fussy about who he partners with and always does background checks on potential partners. Whether family, friends, or business associates, it is very important to him to really know who he is going into business with.

Something very important to take away from how Don creates joint ventures is that no matter who the other party is, he treats it like a business relationship when discussing or dealing with property issues. For example, legal agreements are written and completed, regular meetings are held to discuss any property issues, and these topics are not allowed to enter into any family get-togethers. He also requires the other party to get independent legal and accounting advice before signing any of the agreements.

It's important to treat these relationships very seriously; you are in a trust situation where you are investing other people's money alongside yours. If you wouldn't invest in the deal with your own money, never invest in it with someone else's. Don recommends you "design the divorce in advance"—before you get into a joint venture agreement, make sure you and the other party truly understand what each person's role is to be, how the profits and cash flow will be divided during and at the end of the relationship and, just as importantly, how you are going to deal with the situation if one party does not perform his or her duties or is not able to wait until the agreed sale time. It is much easier to come to an agreement before there is any real money on the table. A well-written agreement will protect your interests should the partnership or deal encounter issues. For example, you need to know what might happen if your joint venture partner gets divorced or dies, and you need to have a plan in place should your exit strategy need to change because of a shift in the real estate cycle.

Before you buy your first property with your new partner, create a spreadsheet that will be used to divide the profits. Use your accountant to ensure that all of the taxes, dividends, and expenses are included in the calculation. Both partners must agree that this will be the template, so there are no disputes in the future. This spreadsheet becomes an integral part of your joint venture agreement.

KEEP YOUR ADVISORS INFORMED

As you and your investors will be relying on trusted tax and legal advisors, you will need to budget for these expenses at the beginning. Engage them early in the process and keep them informed along the way. You will need a legal agreement that clearly defines the relationship and what happens as the deal proceeds. Your tax advisor also needs to know the details of your joint venture deal as both parties will have to file the appropriate reports with the Canada Revenue Agency every year, whether there were any profits or not. Under Canadian tax law, you cannot put strategies in place retroactively.

KEY INSIGHT

Never, ever put someone else's money into a deal if you are not 100-percent sure the deal is a good one, or if the deal is one that you wouldn't put your own money into.

VII INSURANCE AND INVESTMENTS

44

Insure Your Investment

Canadian real estate investors have to take property insurance seriously if they buy a personal residence or investment property in the United States. But how do you know that you're working with a reputable insurance agent and that you are carrying enough insurance? Here are a series of factors to consider to ensure you properly and adequately insure your real estate investments.

FIND AN AGENT WHO CAN SHOP AROUND

Ask the insurance agent questions about his or her history insuring investment properties or second homes for Canadians. There are some real advantages to working with an insurance agent who is capable of writing policies through several different insurance companies. Since different companies offer different insurance packages, this type of agent may be more familiar with market options and is in a better position to review several insurance options before making a recommendation.

The agent should also have experience writing policies for the type of home you need to insure. If you are dealing with single-family homes or multi-family homes, make sure the agent knows what you really need. He or she should be able to anticipate your questions—and present options and scenarios you haven't even considered.

> ## HOME WARRANTY INSURANCE
>
> Before we talk about insurance generally, you should be aware of the home warranty program readily available in the United States. This program covers repairs to the house and repairs or replacement for appliances and air conditioners. If you buy an investment property or second home that is new or just renovated, you should consider this. It is not costly—normally less than $500 per year. For investors, this can be part of the repair and maintenance allowance.

AREAS OF COVERAGE

For rent-and-hold investments and for second homes that are vacant part of the year, you need to focus on the following coverage areas:

- Dwelling
- Other structures
- Personal property
- Loss of use
- Liability
- Medical payments to others
- Replacement cost value and actual cost value

Dwelling

This aspect of the insurance applies to "permanently attached" items, so it typically covers your house and the attached structures and fixtures in the house, such as built-in appliances, plumbing, heating, permanently installed air conditioning systems, and electrical wiring. Some appliances, such as a dishwasher, are considered to be "hardwired" to the property and are therefore included under this coverage. Using the same rationale, a refrigerator would not be covered because it is not permanently attached to the property.

Other Structures

"Other structures" are detached structures such as garages, storage sheds, and fences. If your property has a storage shed, you need to make sure that your policy covers it. This is an area where the wrong assumption can cost you a whole lot of money. Make sure the agent you're talking to has all the necessary information.

Personal Property

This part of your policy typically covers personal property, including the contents of your home and other personal items owned by you or the family members who live with you. This protection can be based on actual cash value or replacement cost. If you are the landlord, you should strongly encourage your tenants to get renter's insurance. Without it, their personal property will not be covered in the event of insurable property loss.

Loss of Use

This covers loss of rental income because of an insurable loss. Let's say your tenant starts a kitchen fire while cooking and the property sustains extensive damage such that the home is no longer habitable. The *loss of use coverage* will cover the loss of rent while the property is being renovated. This sustains your cash flow.

Should the fire occur in your personal second home, loss of use coverage will cover the cost of additional living expenses for you and your family while the property is being renovated.

Liability

Personal liability coverage protects you against a claim or lawsuit resulting from bodily injury or property damage caused to others by an accident on your property. Canadians who own rental property or a second home in the United States must take this coverage seriously. Liability insurance is a critical part of your asset protection plan. See Part 5 for more information on personal liability.

Medical Payments to Others

This pays medical expenses for persons accidentally injured on your property. Considering you now own property in the world's most litigious society, medical payment coverage is another very important way to protect your business.

KEY INSIGHT

Property insurance is one area where cheaper is definitely not better. Some states set relatively low limits for insurance coverage. Don't be taken in. You need good advice about how much insurance is enough. Ask if an umbrella policy makes sense. This is in addition to other insurance and goes "over top" property, automobile insurance, and workers' compensation insurance, for example.

A NOTE ABOUT THE SECOND HOME

Insurance insiders say that a second home typically can be insured under a standard homeowner's policy, which generally offers the best coverage at the best rate. But if you own a second home that you live in for several months of the year and then decide to rent it during the other months, you must notify your agent. The minute you have a tenant in your property, your homeowner's policy will not cover you completely should you have a loss.

REPLACEMENT COST VALUE AND ACTUAL CASH VALUE

When buying insurance, it is important to understand the difference between replacement cost value and actual cash value. *Replacement cost value* (RCV) is the actual cost to replace an item or structure at its pre-loss condition, while *actual cash value* (ACV) is computed by subtracting depreciation from the replacement cost. Costly mistakes often are made if investors fail to ascertain with clarity the terms of their insurance policy with respect to RCV and ACV, so be careful. Let's take a look at an example of what could happen.

Say a windstorm or hurricane destroys the roof on your property. The roof was ten years old and cost $8,000 when it was originally installed. It's going to cost $10,000 to have a new roof installed with roofing material of like kind and quality, such as three-table shingles with a twenty-year life expectancy.

Under an ACV policy, the insurance company is going to determine the depreciation that has occurred to the roof already and subtract it from the replacement cost. Using an industry standard calculation that says three-tab shingles depreciate 5 percent a year, the insurance company will pay out $5,000 for a new roof.

REPLACING THOSE SHINGLES

10-year-old roof that depreciates 5% a year = 50% depreciation withheld

$10,000 cost of new roof − $5,000 depreciation = $5,000 ACV to be paid by insurance company

Under an RCV policy, the insurance company would compensate you the full $10,000 for the new roof. Of course, opting for RCV coverage will increase the cost of your insurance policy, but if you ever need to file a claim, you'll be glad you chose this option. That peace of mind is even more important when your investment property or second home is located a long way away—and in a different country, to boot!

Read Your Policy

Make insurance a cornerstone of your due diligence. Too many people do not read their policies until after they have a loss and need to make a claim. Do your homework up front and avoid nasty surprises!

MAKING A CLAIM

To understand the value of a good insurance policy, it's helpful to look at what happens when you need to make a claim. Here's a quick checklist of what you need to do:

- ❑ Notify your agent immediately. You will want to call and put the agent on notice even if you are unsure if you will make a claim.

- ❑ Take pictures and/or video to document all damages.

- ❑ If at any time you need to undertake any temporary repairs so that you don't incur additional damages, do them.

- ❑ Be sure to take pictures of the temporary repairs and keep all of your receipts.

- ❏ An adjustor from the insurance company will contact you and arrange to inspect the damage. After the adjustor inspects the damages, he will determine what he believes to be the cost of the repairs.

- ❏ Get three independent bids for the repairs, and compare them to the insurance company estimate.

- ❏ If the insurance adjustor estimated the repairs accurately, you will get a settlement to complete the repairs.

The Settlement

The insurance company generally will issue a settlement in one of two ways. The company will either give you a check in the amount they believe the repairs will cost, or will send you their estimate with a sworn proof of loss statement that you will have to sign, have notarized, and send back to the insurance company before you are issued any payment for the loss.

KEY INSIGHT

Be careful what you sign. When you sign this sworn proof of loss statement, you acknowledge that the repairs will cost no more than the insurance company's original estimate. You therefore have no recourse if the repairs cost more or if any additional damage is found.

If your estimates are higher than the estimate used by the insurance company, do not sign the sworn proof of loss statement, which is your prerogative. Instead, submit the three estimates with a letter to the insurance company. The letter should state that the insurance company's estimate is low given your own estimates. Ask the company to review the three estimates you have obtained, and to issue settlement based on the actual costs found in the three estimates. Insurers will typically settle based on the lowest of the three submitted estimates.

LOCATION, LOCATION, LOCATION!

Like automobile insurance the price of property insurance is determined largely by where you live. Hence, the insurance premium for a $150,000 home in one city in Florida will not be the same as a house in another city, let alone another state.

Some of this is because of severe weather like hurricanes, tornadoes, and earthquakes. For example, hurricanes are a reality in Florida and premiums will be higher depending on your property's proximity to the coast. The US Weather Service estimates Jacksonville to be the least likely coastal city to experience hurricane-force winds in any given year with a probability of one in 50. In Miami, it's one in seven thanks to its proximity to the Gulf Stream, which obviously means a higher premium. In California, insurance is affected by the potential for earthquakes.

Myth: Insurance in Florida is far higher than in most states in the United States.

Fact: This is not the case. Insurance in southern Florida is higher because of the increased risk of hurricanes, but that's not an issue in the northern part of the state.

Insurance premiums can affect your investment's cash flow. Since insurance is one area with few "global" truths, get your information from knowledge-able local agents.

45

Carry Insurance Beyond the Property Line: Medical, Auto, and Third-Party Liability

Canadians traveling to the United States as investors or snowbirds must also make sure they carry adequate medical, automobile, and third-party liability insurance, all of which protect them when unforeseen events put their Canadian and US assets at risk. When discussing this coverage with an insurer, make honesty your best policy. Make sure they know the following:

- How long you will be away

- If you plan to travel to the United States often

- If you are taking your own vehicle or renting one

- If you are staying at a hotel or rental home

MEDICAL INSURANCE

Most Canadians know that medical treatment in the United States is expensive, but many do not realize just how expensive it is. Did you know that typical inpatient costs at US hospitals tally more than US$10,000 per night? If you're still not convinced that medical coverage is absolutely necessary, consider one of the stories a US insurance industry colleague shared with us.

A 72-year-old Canadian man took a two-week trip to North Carolina. On the last day of his trip he fainted and was taken to hospital, where doctors treated him for atrial fibrillation. An air ambulance was arranged to return him to Ontario, at a cost of almost C$13,000. This trip included door-to-door service, with ambulance transport to the US airport and then from the Ontario airport to the hospital. The US hospital stay and air ambulance trip added up to more than C$100,000 and were fully covered by his travel medical insurance.

Some Canadian snowbirds and investors say they deliberately skip medical insurance because of the added expense, but this is definitely one instance where it is better to be safe than sorry and to shop around. The policy that covered the Ontario resident in this story cost $150. Here are a few other considerations to keep in mind.

Type of Trip

Travel medical insurance can be purchased for single trips or for multiple trips over the course of a year. The multi-trip plans usually offer coverage for trips up to a specified length of time such as one week, two weeks, one month, or six months, and it pays to go this route if you plan on three trips over the course of a year. Those planning one longer trip are usually better off with the single-trip option.

Financial Coverage

Policies are typically issued for either $2 million or $5 million. They should cover emergency treatment of accidents or illness, including ambulance costs, hospital and doctors' fees, prescription drugs, and rental of medical devices like crutches.

Make sure that your insurance covers things such as air evacuations, the cost of bringing your family members to your bedside, and living expenses for your family while you remain hospitalized. Also, ensure it includes repatriation; you want to make sure that if you die while in the United States, your body is returned to Canada for burial.

Know the Rules for Pre-Existing Conditions

Coverage may still be available if you have a pre-existing condition. You may need to complete a medical questionnaire, but there are very few conditions that can't be covered, especially if you have been stable for the last six months.

Be mindful of the details, because some policies won't cover any pre-existing conditions and the definitions of what constitutes a pre-existing condition may vary from company to company.

KEY INSIGHT

Simply displaying symptoms of an illness is often enough to exclude coverage, even if a diagnosis hasn't been made.

Premiums, Deductibles, and Payment Arrangements

Premiums are often based on a combination of your age and the duration of your travel. Ask your local insurance broker for a breakdown of packages available to you and find out your coverage deductible and the payment arrangements. Will the insurance company pay the hospital directly or will you need to pay and wait for reimbursement?

AUTOMOBILE INSURANCE

Automobile insurers want to know where you're going and for how long. If you are taking your own vehicle, notify your local insurance carrier and the local licensing office as well as the licensing department in the state you are going to visit.

Because provincial laws vary you need to ask your local insurer about specific requirements. For example, if you live in British Columbia, the law says that a vehicle out of the province for vacation purposes does not require any additional coverage. But if you are traveling with the purpose of investing in real estate, the trip is not a vacation, it's business. In British Columbia, you would be required to change the territory your vehicle is licensed in if you are gone more than thirty days.

Some US states may require you to license your vehicle in that state if you are going to remain there for an extended period of time. Do your research.

KEY INSIGHT

Mind the rules. If you are required to license your vehicle in the United States and don't, your Canadian license won't be valid and your Canadian insurance won't help if there's trouble.

Rental Cars

Be extra vigilant if renting a car while you're away. A lot of automobile renters pay the renter way too much for insurance, or don't take the rental agency's "extra coverage" because they think their credit card will protect them.

While some credit cards have sufficient coverage, most do not. They generally provide you with a collision damage waiver only. This does not include any liability or theft coverage nor does it cover loss of use/income for the time that repairs are being done. These are all things you are responsible for when you sign the rental contract.

You can eliminate these issues by buying rental car insurance as an add-on to your regular car insurance, or as a stand-alone policy.

THIRD-PARTY LIABILITY INSURANCE

Third-party liability insurance is another area fraught with misunderstanding. This coverage protects you for damages done to others. A limit of at least C$3 million to C$5 million is advisable in and outside Canada. Never forget that a lot of Americans do not have adequate health insurance. If an accident happens and the court decides *you* caused it, the plaintiff will be after you to cover his or her medical bills. This is definitely one fight you want your insurance company to handle.

KEY INSIGHT

As Canadian courts are awarding ever-higher amounts of money to plaintiffs, third-party liability coverage is no longer a luxury—it's a personal and professional fact of life.

Third-party liability can also be critical if you're in a motor vehicle accident in one of the many states that require motorists to carry insurance or in one that follows some kind of an insurance hybrid approach. For example, while New Hampshire and Virginia do not require insurance at all, California and New Jersey require insurance but set very low minimum limits. Again, that puts your assets at considerable risk, and underlines the importance of carrying adequate liability and medical insurance to make sure that you don't run into any problems after an accident.

Ask your local insurer about the rules in the states you plan to spend time in or drive through. You can get special coverage for "underinsured drivers" that will cover you in states where coverage is not mandatory or is too low.

Appendix: Considerations for Buying a Second Home

We will start with the assumption that you will ensure that you can meet your financial obligations when buying a second property. Considerations of financing costs, closing costs, commissions, utility payments, condo fees, and taxes, together with the costs of traveling to your home, have all been weighed and you have a go on the financial front.

The following lists are some other factors you may want to consider.

Family:

- How many people will be sharing your second home?

- How many bedrooms do you need?

- Are there second apartments available in your complex for family members to rent?

- What kind of activities do you want available for your grandchildren? (Do you want to be near amusement parks, for example?)

Weather:

- What are the weather patterns for the areas you are considering? (Don't forget to think about tornados and hurricanes in the southern United States.)

- What do you want to do at your property and how will the weather affect those plans?

Transportation:

- How are you going to get to your new home?
- Do you want to drive?
- Are there direct flights or will you have to change planes?
- How does a change of planes affect family members who may only be able to visit for a week at a time?

Infrastructure:

- How are you going to get around once you are at your new home?
- Do you need to buy or rent a car?
- Are there bus/train services? Are there accessible taxi services?

Community:

- Do you want to be part of a community?
- Do you want a recreation centre where you can meet other people to share activities like bridge, card games, hobbies?
- Do you want to be near a spa?
- Do you want to co-locate with friends?

Other community factors you might want to think about are the social and political norms in the area, and whether they mesh with your values, or will even affect your living there.

Crime rate and security:

- What are the crime rates like for the community?
- Is there security at the property?
- Do you want to live in a gated community?

Groceries and services:

- Are supermarkets, fresh markets, and organic markets available?
- Are the services and amenities you want for your life accessible and affordable?

- Is there a local labor pool that you can hire from for domestic help, gardening, repairs, and other odd jobs?

Shopping, restaurants, and nightlife:

- Do you want to have easy access to shopping?

- Do you like to eat out a lot?

- Do you want variety in the types of restaurants that are available to you?

- Do you like to cook at home?

- Do you want entertainment venues nearby?

- Do you want to be near a casino?

Outdoor activities:

- Do you play golf?

- Do you play tennis?

- Do you want an indoor/outdoor swimming pool?

- Do you want to hike?

- Do you want to boat and/or fish?

- Do you want to ski?

- What outdoor activities are most important to you and your family?

Cultural activities:

- How important is it to you to have access to the theater, opera, and/or symphony?

- Do you want art galleries and museums to visit?

Natural beauty:

- What appeals to you? The mountains? The beach? The desert? A lake?

Index

About the Authors

Richard Dolan is the managing partner of the Real Estate Investment Network (REIN™) Ltd. and U.S. Property Shop Inc. The U.S. Property Shop provides Canadians with a full suite of services and expertise on purchasing US estate, whether for personal use or investment purposes. Dolan is the author of *Life Rich Real Estate: Matching People with Place* and co-author, with Dr. Paul Stoltz, visiting professor, Harvard Business School, of *The Invincible Investor*.

Don R. Campbell is a founding partner of the Real Estate Investment Network. He is a leader in providing current real estate investment education programs and economic research materials; author of the best-selling *Real Estate Investing in Canada 2.0;* and co-author of *97 Tips for Canadian Real Estate Investors, Real Estate Joint Ventures*, and *Secrets of the Canadian Real Estate Cycle*.

David Franklin, B.Comm., JD, is chairman and chief legal counsel for REIN. Franklin serves as the U.S. Property Shop's cross-border tax and legal expert on real estate and estate planning.